DREAMING
OF STEAM

23 tales of Wolds and rails

DREAMING OF STEAM

23 tales of Wolds and rails

First Published 2017 by Fantastic Books Publishing

Cover photograph 1958 Heading for Burdale Tunnel from Driffield
© www.transporttreasury.co.uk

Cover design by Gabi Grubb

ISBN (eBook): 9781912053704
ISBN (paperback): 9781912053698

Dedication

This collection is dedicated to the thousands of fans and enthusiasts who tirelessly work to preserve the railway heritage of the British Isles and beyond.

Acknowledgements

With special thanks to the Board of the Yorkshire Wolds Railway for supporting this collection; and to the Authors' Licensing and Collecting Society for its untiring work on behalf of authors and for its generous sponsorship of the Dreaming of Steam project.

Contents

Foreword

by Lord Faulkner of Worcester

Writing in his novel Sybil in 1848 Disraeli said 'The railways will do as much for mankind as the monasteries did.' Part of that contribution has been the railways' contribution to literature, with great writers like Dickens and Conan Doyle putting railways centre stage in their books and short stories.

The competition that formed the basis for this first-class anthology accords perfectly with this great tradition. I commend the initiative of Fantastic Books Publishing and the Yorkshire Wolds Railway in finding such an excellent and innovative way to bring the rich heritage of their railway to a wider audience. The range of short stories was truly fascinating: from supernatural and science-fiction to wartime drama and accounts based on real people and events.

It particularly pleased me to see so many authors mining a rich seam of history from the Malton to Driffield line's early 20th century past, when three trains a day in each direction (and a fourth on Tuesdays, Thursdays and Saturdays) meandered their way across the Wolds, taking 45 to 50 minutes to cover the 20 miles from Malton to Driffield. Many stories in this collection hark back to this period, opening windows on the lives of the people who lived in the beautiful Yorkshire Wolds in those turbulent times, especially during the cataclysmic years of the 1914-18 war.

I especially applaud the work of the Yorkshire Wolds Railway project that has not only restored a running locomotive to a line closed 50 years ago, but that has diversified into projects such as this anthology to spread the word and keep alive the history and spirit of such an important area of our heritage.

You don't need to be a railway enthusiast to enjoy this stunning collection of stories, and I hope that the passion within these pages fires your imagination and spurs you to put Wetwang and the Yorkshire Wolds on your itinerary for a visit.

Richard Faulkner is President of the Heritage Railway Association and a member of the Government's world war one centenary advisory board. He was the co-author of the award-winning Holding The Line – How Britain's Railways Were Saved, and Disconnected! Broken Links in Britain's Rail Policy.

March 2017

A Solicitous Wife

by Madeleine McDonald

This story was highly commended by the competition judges

Sledmere and Fimber. Copyright © A M Ross

'I say, your skirt's rather short, isn't it?'

Elizabeth repressed a sigh. If only Mama had explained how difficult life with a husband would be. 'Shorter skirts are practical, Richard. We are taking the train today and I find it far easier to climb in and out of the carriage dressed like this.' She demonstrated by lifting the skirt free of her ankles and raising each knee in turn.

A month earlier, as a bride, she would have pirouetted in her new outfit for Richard's approval. In that month she had learned to suppress spontaneity.

'As you wish,' he said. 'But my mother never complained.' In the doorway, he turned back. His eyes were fond. 'You always look charming to me. But I have a reputation to consider. It would not do for people to say my wife looks fast.'

'No, dearest.'

Before her marriage, Elizabeth had taken her problems to Frances. War committee work took up all Mama's time and her younger sister's new governess treated her like a grown-up. However, Frances was unmarried. It was impossible to ask her advice now.

Richard's proposal had come as a surprise, for he was a business acquaintance of her father. Papa pointed out the advantages of the match, when peace had brought further upheaval and so many young men had not come home from the trenches. Elizabeth knew she could not afford to be choosy. Before her eyes was the example of dear Frances, trapped in spinsterhood at 26. Richard might be a generation older, but he was established in his profession, and offered financial security. Also, he seemed a kind man.

Running upstairs to find a hat, Elizabeth reflected that Richard might have a point. A solicitor's wife was always in the public eye, and he was well known in Malton. She hesitated between last year's cloche and the latest sporty beret style. The day did promise to be warm, but would Richard call a beret fast, especially one embroidered in red? He was unpredictable. She chose the cloche and found a loose cardigan to go over her new skirt, rather than the matching coat the seamstress had delivered.

By the time they had walked to Wetwang station, any discontent had evaporated. She loved their trips to Malton market, and never tired of the views from the train window. City bred, and accustomed to the grime of Leeds, the open, rolling country of the Wolds had been a revelation. The villages lay hidden in hollows, protected from winter's blasts. From the train, the seemingly bare landscape lacked the dark grandeur of the Pennines, but entranced her all the more for that. Trees were rare, and try as she might, she could see no corner that had not been tilled or cultivated. Today, the huge, sloping fields were golden with corn. In some, the reapers were already at work, walking behind the binder and stacking the sheaves into stooks. Elizabeth tugged at Richard's sleeve whenever she saw it was a tractor that pulled the binder.

'Look, there's another one.' The snub-nosed tractors, with their small front wheels and huge back ones, fascinated her. She had once been for a ride in a motor car and found it thrilling.

Richard rustled his newspaper. 'Progress, some would say. I'm sorry to see the horses go, myself, but the farmers tell me one machine does twice the work of a team of horses. With the price of wheat falling they have no choice.'

Elizabeth went back to staring out of the window.

~

Two passengers alighted at Sledmere, leaving them alone in their first class carriage.

Richard put down his newspaper and coughed. 'As you know, I consulted Doctor Carroll last week. He suggested I keep a record of my irregularity. I shall rely on you to keep the record up to date, and co-ordinate it with your choice of menus.'

Elizabeth stared. What was this new wifely duty? She was aware she still had much to learn. Mama had informed her about a husband's expectations and, truth to tell, Elizabeth found the intimate side of marriage more enjoyable than she expected. It also put Richard in a good mood, which was another excellent reason to encourage his attentions.

'What do you mean, dearest?'

His tone was brisk. 'I went this morning, for the first time in four days. You may start with that.'

'Oh, you mean …you mean ...?'

'A call of nature, yes, Elizabeth. As my wife, you are expected to take a close interest in my health. Carroll says bodily hygiene is most important for a man. Irregularity can be uncomfortable as well as injurious to health.'

Elizabeth retrieved her diary from her capacious handbag. It seemed the most appropriate place to record the startling information. The train jolted, and her pencil streaked across the page. 'Four days, yes. It is noted. Should I also write down what medicine you are taking?'

'Senna, liquorice and–' He broke off. 'What on earth are those squiggles?'

'Shorthand. I don't know how well I will read it back, the train is jolting me so, but I will remember.' Pride in her accomplishments loosened her tongue. Richard must surely approve of a clever wife. 'In case one of the servants should happen to find my diary, dearest, I know you would prefer such details to be kept private, as a matter between you and me.' She showed him the page. 'See. My sister's governess taught me shorthand. It is a most intriguing system. Does your clerk write shorthand? I understand it is most useful in business.'

'Certainly not. He writes an excellent copperplate hand.'

'Frances, our governess, learned it because she thought women would need to earn their own money after the war. And that is true. I hear there are now young ladies who take employment as typewriters.'

Richard frowned. 'But they are not from families such as yours. Do your parents know she holds such views? Is she one of those tiresome suffragettes?'

'Of course not,' Elizabeth lied, reflecting that votes for women was another subject of conversation to avoid in future. Marriage was indeed a minefield. She distracted Richard by stroking his hand. In private, he showed a remarkable readiness to respond to her advances and it was a most useful way of changing the subject. 'Remember, dearest, it is my destiny to be interested in the modern world. I was born in the new century.'

Richard stroked her hand in turn. 'True. An old man like me is lucky to have you.'

Late in the afternoon, when they returned to Wetwang, Elizabeth stole a nasturtium flower from the station display. In the privacy of her bedroom, she tucked the flower into her diary as a marker. Her fingers caressed the embossed cover as she put it away.

Her innermost thoughts would be safe. In shorthand, her diary would be as impenetrable to her husband as if written in Ancient Greek. He would be content that she was keeping a daily record of his health, as a good wife should.

Trains of Thought

by Alan Paine

This story was awarded the Julia Bradbury prize
for capturing the spirit of the Wolds

Fairy Dale. Copyright ©R M Dixon

The artist sat on the hill taking in the scene before him. It was such a pleasant sunny day that he was tempted to lie down and top up his tan rather than following his original plan. The smooth curve of the valley below seemed to have been carved by a careful hand but had in fact been gouged out by the blind force of a glacier thousands of years before. The white face of the quarry shone in the middle distance, a very deliberate man-made feature of the landscape.

His brightest cerulean blue swiftly captured the glorious summer sky. Successively paler shades of green and grey swept the Wolds landscape out away from him. Simulating the roughness of the quarry and the swirl of the surrounding trees with textured acrylic paint was the most fun part but he paused as his gaze traced the line of the old track bed, where the railway had crossed the land before it had been closed in the 1950s. It would be wonderful to put that life back into the scene, a train just disappearing around the bend behind the quarry.

Working on his sketch pad and even studying pictures he brought up on his phone he couldn't find a way to give the impression of a railway line without trying to show every detail which would be impossible unless he had a much bigger canvas. He toyed with the idea of going home to work on the painting but he really wanted to finish it here and now in situ and he pressed on trying to figure out what to do.

'Hello,' said a voice behind him.

He looked round with a start and saw a pretty young woman in her late teens or early twenties in a red and white floral dress with her brown hair tied back in a simple pony tail. He was afraid she had come to tell him that he was trespassing. It had been difficult to get to where he was because the area was mostly surrounded by fences and cultivated land. But she simply came and sat beside him.

'That's a nice painting.' She leaned across him, peering intently at the half finished canvas. 'I'm Marjorie. I live on a farm just over there,' she continued, still studying the painting and waving vaguely in no particular direction.

'Peter,' said the artist. 'And thank you.'

'Nice to meet you, Peter.' She smiled and grasped his hand.

Before he could reply, she went on, 'I used to come up here a lot with my boyfriend. 'It was love at first sight for both of us, you know.' Peter opened his mouth to respond politely, but Marjorie launched into a detailed description of how she had been out cycling one day and had seen Tomasz working in the fields picking vegetables. He'd noticed her too but Tomasz was Polish and spoke very little English.

'I couldn't speak Polish at all of course, but with a few words of English and some pictures on bits of paper we managed to meet up from time to time. Sometimes he'd even sneak away from work while his mates covered for him.

'We were both interested in painting,' she went on, 'and we would sit up here doing watercolours and ...'

He glanced at her as she paused and saw the blush creep up her neck.

'A girl has to be careful,' she said. 'Even these days.'

Peter thought that this was a strange remark but decided it best not to follow it up. 'I don't know how farmers are going to get Eastern European workers after Brexit,' he said trying to steer the conversation in a hopefully less personal direction.

She looked at him blankly. 'He was killed a few months after we met in an accident at a level crossing near Driffield along with two other workers. When I heard the news I came up here and cried from afternoon to the next morning.'

Peter felt awkward. He remembered hearing about a number of accidents at level crossings in East Yorkshire and wondered which one it had been. He didn't know what to say to her. He looked at her gazing wistfully into the distance and then turned away.

'I just can't work out how to show a train going along the old railway line,' he said finally.

Marjorie seemed to brighten. 'Can I have a go?'

'Sure.' He smiled, offering her the sketch pad. But before he could stop her, she made for the canvas and began rapidly dabbing away with a brush. He was about to protest but then, as if by magic, he saw an amazing representation of the track emerging. A subtle blur in the background getting gradually more detailed until Peter could almost count the sleepers where the line entered the tunnel below the hill. Then she added two red and white coaches pulled by a black steam locomotive puffing out a huge trail of smoke behind it. She had perfectly judged the scale as if she'd been tracing a photograph.

Peter was outraged that she had attacked his work like that but her contribution fitted so well with what he had done that he couldn't help but be impressed.

'That's ...' His mind battled over the words *fantastic* and *outrageous*, and ended on a sigh.

'I'll be off then,' she said, turning and heading up the dale.

Peter watched her until the red and white of her dress merged into a single colour and finally, disappeared from sight. He turned back to the canvas and busied himself with completing the work, concentrating intensely. In the hot sun it didn't take long for the picture to dry and, with satisfaction, he wrote, 'Burdale from Fairy Dale August 2016,' on the back.

When he looked around again, something was wrong. The sun had gone, and in the greying valley a chill was coming. Could it really be almost dusk? He turned back to the painting and was puzzled by what he saw. The track and train were clearly in his own hand, clumsy and out of proportion compared with Marjorie's perfect touch. And he'd splashed multi-coloured blobs of paint right in the middle of the hillside where he was sure that it had been perfect.

He peered closer and as he looked again the blobs almost seemed to be people. He stared at the shapes on the hillside that hovered between people and random splodges. He thought he saw a woman in a red and white dress and a man in a dark coloured shirt half hidden in the grass.

Slowly turning over the canvas, his confusion became cold shock when he saw written on the back in his own handwriting, 'Marjorie and Tomasz in Fairy Dale, August 1948.'

It didn't take long to find the faded black and white pictures on his phone. The tangled burnt out wreck of the lorry in which Polish and Hungarian farm workers had been travelling was barely recognisable but the steam locomotive which had struck it stood unscathed on the track exactly as Marjorie had shown it.

A Tartan Rug

by Colin Hollis

This story was long listed by the competition judges

Burdale station. Copyright © W R Burton Author's Collection

'Heaven,' she said. 'What would your version of heaven look like?'

He turned on the bench to look at her, but she was watching the raindrops running down the glass, combining, merging, splitting, reforming. 'You do know that there's no room in my philosophy for a heaven, don't you?'

'Don't be silly. Of course I do. It's just a game. Humour me. Tell me what a heaven would look like for you.'

They were shoulder to shoulder and he leaned away slightly. When he spoke with any enthusiasm, he made shapes with his hands and he didn't want his movements to disturb her. He found the words quickly. 'Right. Heaven. A town, or quiet part of a small city, old stone, lots of terracotta. There's a strong Mediterranean feel, and some antiquity to it, but I'd still like it to be in Britain. The streets are wet but almost steaming as they dry in early hot sun. It's June; it's always June in heaven.'

They'd set off to walk to town, but the rain had intensified and they'd run to the bus-stop to sit on the narrow metal bench in the shelter. The first bus along would decide whether they went on or went back.

There was a leak in the roof and he reached out his foot to let the drops bounce off his shoe. 'A large paved square, a market square some days, but not today. Today is quiet. There's a couple of coffee shops, newsagent, bakery, florist and such around the outside. The palette is predominately warm tones: honey and apricot, and the terracotta. One of the coffee shops has large umbrellas, blue, the colour of the sky, though I sit out in the sun at my favourite table, with a view of the square and some of the surrounding streets and alleys. There are large pots and troughs of plants about and bicycles leaning on walls. I have a folded newspaper and a paperback in front of me, and a tall glass of fruit juice. From inside the shop I can hear soft music, classical guitar. A few folk are crossing the square to go to work. But not me; I've got all the day for myself.'

He put his hands on his knees and turned his head again, and saw that she was watching him with that nearly smile of hers. 'I can picture it,' she said. 'Any smells?'

He took a while, watched a car pass by, spraying rainwater in arcs. 'No, I'll have to work on that. Yours? What does your heaven look like?'

She was back to watching the raindrops, intently, as if reading a message therein. Her words came slowly at first, careful and precise. 'I'm on a hillside,' she said. 'Gentle, rounded, just below the summit.

14

Neat sheep-cropped grass, but there are areas of meadow all around, wild grasses, daisies, patches of poppies, a scattering of cornflowers. Gentle distant birdsong, with two skylarks so far above, they're almost out of sight. It's sunny and warm, a blue sky with a few, very white, fair-weather clouds.' Without looking, she reached for his hand. 'I wonder if everyone's heaven is sunny.'

'I doubt it. Some heavens will be inside, or at night time.' Her hand was cold and he cupped it in both of his and lifted it to his mouth to breathe his warm air on to it.

She turned and slipped in her other hand and they were facing each other, and very close. 'There's a stream along the bottom, lined with trees, and some woodland scattered about. It's not too high. Just enough for a pleasant walk, and with a big sky, and far enough for no traffic noise.'

'Not the Dales or the moors, then?'

'Not quite. Something a bit softer for me, more gentle. Not so rugged and rocky. That pleasant countryside feel, with nicely curved shapes and an almost random pattern of fields in their early summer colours. A few fences and corners of stone wall and hedgerows, but not too many boundaries, not too many enclosures. A couple of stiles and a kissing gate would work.'

A small motorcycle passed, its rider's head down and hunched. He tilted his gaze to follow it, and when he turned back, she was watching him.

'There's a path from the bottom, and a few walkers scattered along it, but it's off to the side. A dad and his daughter are flying a kite. And yes, it's June.'

She stopped then, and he fastened his focus on her eyes, and she opened them wide, knowing that he enjoyed looking into them.

'Your heaven,' he said. 'What time of day is it?'

'Early afternoon. We've just had lunch, a picnic, and packed away and can now doze in the sun.'

'We?'

'Me and you. It wouldn't be my heaven without you. We'll go together.' She closed her eyes. 'We've got one of those good quality tartan rugs and a nice bag for the picnic. You'd better bring a backpack so that I can have a headrest when I lie down.'

She smiled at him. 'And no tickling my nose with a blade of grass when I'm falling asleep.'

He shook his head. 'I wouldn't do that,' a serious tone to his voice.

They were quiet for a long time. 'I can find that for you,' he said. 'I know just the place.'

'Really?'

'Wharram. The Yorkshire Wolds. We went there from school. There's an ancient deserted village. Wharram Percy. It's near Malton.'

'Close enough to Malton to walk?'

'I don't know, we went by coach. I'll look it up. Perhaps we should have a car. They're going to revive an old railway. The Yorkshire Wolds Railway. Perhaps we can use that.'

'Will it have steam engines, with puffs of white smoke and that lovely chugging sound and a tooty whistle?'

'I hope so.'

The rain had almost stopped and the sky was brightening.

'Good. We'll go there a few times a year. Forever.'

'Not just in June?'

'No. I'd like to visit in different seasons.'

'Shouldn't we live in a cottage nearby?'

'No need,' she said. 'The visits will be enough. Though I'll not refuse the cottage if it happens.' She stood up and pulled him with her. 'Here comes the bus. Looks like we're going to town. Let's buy the tartan rug today. We'll feel we've made a start.'

They ran across the road for the bus, he holding one hand above her head to protect her from the last drops of rain.

Sunday Sleeper

by Ron Elsdon

This story was long listed by the competition judges

Burdale Tunnel. Copyright © Len Cook

I should not, I suppose, have partaken of such a large lunch. Could it have been simple gluttony or, more intriguingly, some sort of benevolent prompting? I know which the obvious answer is, but I also know which one I prefer. The events of such an unforgettable Sunday afternoon are clear in my mind.

I stop at an Italian restaurant in Cottingham, where I am seduced by the menu, enticing me to succumb to the succulent delights of a rather large calzone pizza and an equally decadent tiramisu. Suitably satiated, I order a strong coffee to help keep me awake and alert for the coming afternoon. I return to the car, belt myself in, and proceed north into the gently rolling slopes of the Yorkshire Wolds, wonderfully lit by a late summer sun reigning supreme in a cloudless sky. I have no journey plan, sometimes I turn right, sometimes left, and sometimes I just go straight on. I wish simply to be in the Wolds.

Cuisine and climate conspire to make me feel sleepy. It has been a long and hectic week at work, after all, but I need to get this car off the road and parked somewhere safe. I pass what looks like a green diesel locomotive in a field behind a hedge. Have I already fallen asleep? Then I see a sign saying, 'Yorkshire Wolds Railway' and another inviting me to turn right into a little car park.

Motivated by self-preservation, I drive in and park alongside a dozen or so other cars. A short section of railway track presents itself, running past a sign proclaiming this to be Fimber Halt. There in front of me is the diesel locomotive, complete with yellow and black nose, red buffer beam and black buffers, it carries a cheeky blue sign on the front announcing it as the 'Malton Dodger'.

A number of people mill about a small refreshment kiosk. Others watch the Dodger. I should get out of the car. Fresh air and a walk will clear the fuzz in my head, but the invitation to close my eyes for a few moments is irresistible. Time for a walk later ...

When I awaken I am, of course, in the same place, but the scene has shifted. The station sign is much larger and tells me that I am at 'Sledmere and Fimber'. I see a proper platform and a station building, a signal box and signals. And there is a railway track stretching away into the distance in both directions.

People crowd the platform, shouting, talking animatedly on their phones, pulling out cameras. There is excitement in the air. Something is afoot, something big.

Refreshed by my forty winks, I climb out of the car and make my way to the heart of the crowd. Folk are glad to enlighten me. A special train is due.

Gears shift in my mind. Fimber can't be just a length of track, but a station on a through route. I ask a bright-eyed woman.

'Yes,' she assures me. 'This is a proper railway now. It runs from Driffield to Malton just like it used to.' She chats on about the good old days before transport ministers redrew the railway map and before anyone had ever heard of a certain Dr Beeching.

I look in the direction of the signal box. Silhouetted through the windows against a bright sky, the signalman is on the move, pulling levers with some vigour. I can clearly hear them as they slam into place. I look south. The arm on one of the signals rotates upwards with a faint 'clank'. The buzz in the crowd around me rises to a new level. The excitement is intense and I am not immune.

I kick myself for setting off this morning without my trusty camera.

A moment later the buzz takes a new tone. Everyone is looking south.

We all hear it, the sustained and rich tone of a steam locomotive whistle. Then there is smoke and steam and the eagerly awaited train approaches.

It grows in noise and size, drowning out the crowd's collective sigh as it roars past. A huge cheer erupts, then the locomotive is racing north into the distance and its whistle can be only faintly heard. The smells of hot metal, steam and smoke linger in the air, stirring memories of a previous age. People gather in groups to compare their photographs, some are exhilarated, some deflated. With so many people on the platform, it is a matter of luck whether they snapped the train or other people's heads.

Was I dreaming? No, it really was Flying Scotsman steaming past us and disappearing into the distance. No wonder so many people turned up. What has made the occasion so special is that they only heard about it earlier today. The grand old lady was chartered to haul a special train from London to Scarborough, taking the customary route and only leaving the Great Northern main line at York. Then, disaster threatened: the line west of Malton was blocked by a malfunctioning level crossing. Rather than disappoint the passengers who had paid a small fortune to travel on the train, the powers-that-be pulled out all the stops and rerouted the train via Selby. The recently re-opened Driffield to Malton line saved the day.

I return to my car, happy, and bathed in the exhilaration of the crowd on the platform at Sledmere and Fimber station. A queue is already straining at the leash, eager to be away to speed north to view the train again further up the line. But I am in no hurry. I close my eyes for a few minutes while I wait.

When I awaken I am, of course, in the same place, but the scene has shifted again. I am no longer at Sledmere and Fimber station, I am at Fimber Halt. I see a small green diesel locomotive, proclaiming itself to be the 'Malton Dodger', rumbling down a short section of track.

A few people are drinking coffee at a small kiosk, others are milling about by an information kiosk and some have their cameras trained on the Dodger. There is no station, no platform, no signal box and no signals. It has all been a dream.

I look at my watch. Time has passed. Pulling out of the nearly-empty car park, I turn south and head for home. As I drive, I wonder what to make of my dream in the car park at Fimber Halt. I see two possibilities. One is that it has been the product of an over-active imagination inflamed by a substantial lunch. The other is that I have been afforded a benevolent glimpse into the future. I know which the obvious answer is, but I also know which one I prefer.

Dodging to a Halt

by Janet Batty

This story was highly commended by the competition judges

Sledmere and Fimber. Copyright © W R Burton Author's Collection

As she stood in the old carriage at the newly named Fimber Halt, May gazed at the black and white photograph. It was almost as if the long retired loco was stirring itself to transport her back to that Tuesday in July 1948, over 65 years ago.

May had woken early and dressed quickly in her neatly pressed clothes, laid out on her chair the night before. Her mum had swept back her hair and plaited it tightly, securing it with two blue, satin ribbons. May scarcely had time to finish her breakfast before they were bundled into the car and taken to stand with other families and railway workers awaiting the arrival. The line had been cleared of all other traffic that day.

Right on time, and with a great flourish of steam, the engine 'Irish Elegance' drew up at the station. The bystanders cheered and waved as King George VI and a smiling Queen Elizabeth alighted from the carriage, closely followed by their youngest daughter.

May gasped at the stylishness of their dress, the beautiful lines of Queen Elizabeth's outfit, the smart cut of the King's suit and their daughter …What May would give for shoes like that!

The royal party walked purposely along the platform to be greeted by Sir Richard and Lady Sykes, who would accompany them on the short drive to Sledmere House. May's father said that they would probably be going to see the racehorses at some point during their stay. As the royal party was whisked away, the onlookers lingered to watch as the engine was shunted into a siding to await their return the next morning. May's head was a whirl of images and sounds as she rode back to the farm in the car. She couldn't wait to tell her friends all about the special visitors.

The steam clouds of memory continued to clear and May now saw herself on a station platform. It was a few months later, September of the same year, thoughts of the royal visit had faded, and May was waiting at Wetwang station. Having left behind the securities of the small village school, she had moved on to a school in Malton. By the start of her second week she was setting off with a growing feeling of independence, wondering what the days ahead would hold before she returned on Friday evening. The Malton Dodger pulled into the station and May climbed into the carriage, waving goodbye to her mother from the open window.

The train pressed on through the familiar scenery of the chalk valley, with the smell of newly cut corn and the sights of harvest all around. As the train pulled into Burdale station, May craned her neck to see if her friend Edith was waiting on the platform. As they ground to a shuddering halt, Edith and her mother emerged from the lean-to extension which served as both waiting room and booking office. Edith clambered up and greeted May enthusiastically and they both waved to Edith's mother as the train set off slowly on the next stage of the journey.

With barely contained excitement, they passed the lone sentinel of Tunnel Cottage. The carriage lights were about to come on and they would hear the announcement to close the windows. They were approaching Burdale tunnel. Today they were the only two passengers in their carriage towards the rear of the train, and as an act of defiance they left the windows open, knowing that in a few minutes the steam would rush in to throw the carriage into an ethereal haze of uncertainty and intrigue. May wondered as they passed through what seemed like the depths of the earth what would happen if the train were to break down? She pushed away a variety of unnerving scenarios as a glimmer of light appeared, heralding the end of the tunnel. She smiled at Edith as the steam cleared and the September sunshine flooded back into the carriage.

As they arrived at Wharram, their attention was drawn to the unusual hive of activity as the newly painted wooden name board was being ceremoniously hoisted on to the station building, following the precise directions of the Station Master. May knew that this was a long-anticipated event. All the enamel name boards had been removed during the war. It seemed a strange precaution to May in those early post-war years, but in 1940 the fear of an invasion had been real. The train moved on, stopping at North Grimston and Settrington, before finally reaching its destination in Malton. May and Edith climbed down and made their way to school to start a new week.

Over the next two years May and Edith became inseparable friends. They grew to love the journey, travelling to school on a Monday morning, to spend the week in boarding accommodation, and then home again on Friday evening. They sat at 'their' two seats as often as they could secure them, looking askance at any unwitting passenger who might get to them first. But this particular journey was possible only for two years, as in June 1950 the line was closed to passengers.

As the two friends walked into the station at Malton on that final Friday evening, the train was ready for departure. The black engine gleamed in the evening sun, dressed in its Sunday best, thought May, just as she had been that momentous Tuesday of the royal visit. She looked at the proud British Railways livery of a lion astride a wheel displayed in red and gold. She had always thought it too majestic for the silly nickname of the 'Cycling Lion'.

Standing beside the humming, hissing engine, she looked up at her ferocious companion and wondered if she would see him again.

'Hurry up!' a voice called down the platform and the girls climbed aboard. They jostled along the busy aisle and after stowing their small cases safely overhead, sank down triumphantly into *their* seats for the last time. They were amazed at the number of people boarding the train to Driffield, and all other destinations between. There would be no leaving the carriage window open when they passed through the tunnel tonight.

The train seemed to be going slowly today as it laboured to climb to Wharram and on to Burdale and the infamous tunnel. It was almost as if it sensed the end of an era and was trying to forestall the inevitable march of time. But the train did finally emerge into the light and the girls hugged farewell. 'See you at Sledmere for the bus on Monday morning,' called May as Edith jumped down on to the platform. 'And don't be late!'

The train groaned into action again and began to build up a head of steam, rattling on towards its final destination. When it pulled into Wetwang, May's father was there to meet her along with a small group of villagers. They had all gathered to watch the train on its penultimate journey. May pushed the last ticket deep into the pocket of her school coat to keep it safe as she climbed down to meet her father.

'Good week, lass?' May nodded. 'That's t'last time tha'll be on t'Malton Dodger.'

Her father's sad gaze followed the train drawing slowly out of the station. May felt the unusual quiet of the watching villagers. Even the railway workers paused to watch as the engine picked up speed.

A sudden sharp whistle made May jump. Sir Tatton Sykes, the new Malton Dodger, announced its presence on the newly laid rails. It was almost as though it had called to her from across the years. She had lost track of time, caught between two worlds. She realised as she looked at the old photographs that she could recall so many sights and sounds of this journey – a journey she had last made over sixty years ago. She sat down in the carriage and opened her handbag to take out the letter.

It was with surprise that she had opened the reply postmarked July 2016, to reveal the crisp white paper and the message which read, 'Thank you for your letter including the delightful photograph from 1948. It clearly captures a special moment in the life of my great-grandmother. I note with interest the information about the revival of the Yorkshire Wolds Railway. Maybe at some point in the future members of my family will have the pleasure of visiting this railway and the Yorkshire Wolds, just as my great-grandparents did so many years ago. I wish you every success in your on-going venture and would be pleased to hear how your project progresses over the coming years ...'

May noted the flourish of the royal signature as she carefully folded the letter and replaced it in her handbag next to a faded old ticket. Could it possibly happen? Perhaps down the proverbial line, she thought with a smile. She looked up again at the photograph of that special visit displayed on the wall of the old carriage. She imagined what her dear father would have said. 'Tha nivver knaws, lass. Tha nivver knaws!'

Hibernaculum

by Lucy Bilton

Lucy Bilton is an invited contributor to this collection

Burdale Tunnel. Copyright © Lime Photographic

Toby wore the meaningful tattoos and tan of a summer spent finding himself in Thailand. Professor Winter knew this from Toby's wholly unnecessary introductory email. It had begun with '*Hey there,*' and the Professor's lip curled in disdain at the memory of it.

The young man now stood in the windowless office of the Zoology Department, propping up the wall with a sandaled foot. He was Professor Winter's new PhD student.

'Look Prof ...' He ran his hand through his bleached hair. 'I know it's a great idea. The site is perfect. Hell, it used to *be* a research site. It'd be awesome for my thesis. I really don't see the problem.'

'The problem, Mr Denton, is simple enough,' said the Professor, removing his glasses and rubbing them slowly with a paisley cloth. 'The Health and Safety Executive closed down the Bat Research Programme in Burdale Tunnel in 1971. No process, no warning, no reply to our reasoned protests.' Winter's rubbing became slightly more urgent though his voice stayed level. 'Overnight it had become too much of a hazard apparently. The old tunnel was always unsafe, that's why the public were not allowed inside, but the university had managed it carefully. God knows what it's like now it has been left to rot. There've been some roof falls since then, completely sealing off the middle section. The HSE feel vindicated I'm sure. The bats can still take refuge there of course, but it's of no use to us.'

He did not add that he had almost failed his third year when his tutor took very unkindly to the sudden shut down of the project and had left without notice or trace.

Professor Winter stood up. 'Look if you don't mind, I've got terrible first year papers to read.' He gestured at the door. 'I suggest you find another scheme to make your mark on the Department. Perhaps try something radical like, oh I don't know, getting published this term?'

Toby shrugged, raised two hands in mock defeat and backed out of the office.

'No worries, Prof. Understood.'

Once outside, Toby raised his middle finger to the office door then headed towards the library.

⁓

At 2.00 am, two nights later, Toby Denton stood at the north portal of Burdale tunnel. He had parked his jeep half a mile away and picked his way through the trees guided by his helmet light. Now he perched on a mossy concrete buttress, his head dipped over the schematics he had purloined from the university archives.

He looked for a moment at the bricked up tunnel mouth, pockmarked with bat holes. The north side felt less exposed somehow. The south portal was an imposing stone-worked double track opening but the money had run low well before the construction reached the north portal. In just under a mile of tunnel, a journey from hubris to humility could be traced, or perhaps simply the age-old story of ambition dissolving to reality.

Toby was a young man unused to having limits, practical or financial, placed on his schemes. He had a selective respect for the word 'no'. The decision to look at the tunnel had been taken before he'd even knocked at the Professor's office door. Damn it, he was qualified to instruct five different extreme sports in three different continents. This was nothing.

Arrogant though he was, Toby was not an idiot. He took measures to mitigate the risk on covert solo expeditions. That was why he had sent a time-stamped email which would only be delivered if he was not back by 9.00 am to cancel the command. He'd had difficulty choosing a recipient though. His new housemates were undergrads and had yet to arrive in Hull. His parents were on the yacht in Martinique, or was it St Barts? Either way, they were of little use.

He gathered his kit and headed into the woods to find the second ventilation shaft which led straight to the sweet spot, the sealed section in the middle of the tunnel. Circling the right co-ordinates, he scanned the ground with his powerful torch. The corner of the concrete cap caught Toby's trained base-jumper's eye. He kicked away the forest mulch and his boot made contact with rusted bars. It would be an easy climb for someone of his experience. The metal grate did not withstand much force from the small crowbar and in a few moments he was abseiling down the inside of the vent.

The atmosphere inside the tunnel was still but not stale. He had braced himself for an assault of dank stagnant air but the environment was not unpleasant. He tugged on his rope instinctively and felt it taught and secure. He would not be down here long, this was just a scoping exercise so that he could make his case to the university and whichever bureaucrats were stopping professional zoologists from putting this abandoned landmark to good use.

It was pitch black inside the sealed section. He shone the torch behind him to inspect the debris from the northern roof fall. But there was no crumbled brick or crushed earth. Just a smooth concrete surface which filled the bore from floor to roof, creating a far more effective seal than any collapse could have made. Toby swung the torch the other way but the beam tapered into the black.

Suddenly from out of the dark, a metallic echo. Toby automatically pressed his back to the wall, his subconscious reminding him of where he was before his conscious reasoned that there had been no trains through here in over 60 years. His palms felt suddenly clammy inside his gloves as he moved down the tunnel into the shadow. The noise came again. It was certainly not a bat. In fact there was no evidence of bats at all. He could only assume that another wall of concrete sealed the other end of the section, not letting anything fly in or out. He moved onwards, tracing the subtle bend of the tunnel. Suddenly an object reared up in front of him, flooded in a pool of shaking torch light.

Toby let out an involuntary laugh. What the hell was this still doing here? A carriage sat on the old track. But this was not an old British Rail carriage, or any other type of carriage he had seen before. It was a steel, windowless box set on wheels. It was certainly not built for passengers and there was no discernable way for goods to get inside. Toby stood open mouthed at the strange metal object sitting like a silent Minotaur at the centre of a dark maze.

He circled the carriage slowly, looking for a door or a hatch.

Nothing. The sides were smooth and impenetrable. As he stepped forward to touch the cold metal, he felt his foot drop and he stumbled. There was a shallow pit beneath it. Without missing a beat, Toby crouched to look at the underside of the carriage and saw a trap door. It was open a crack. He tried it tentatively, letting it swing back shut. The clang of metal on metal echoed through the tunnel's chamber.

He let the echo subside before pushing the trap door again. He climbed warily inside and flicked a switch on the wall in front of him. With a fluorescent hum, the carriage was flooded with harsh white light. Where seats should have been were rows and rows of tightly packed dusty black filing cabinets. They were all identical except for the first. The thick layer of dust had been disturbed by a hand print and a drawer left open. Curiosity won the battle with risk and Toby reached inside. He pulled out a yellowing paper file. He saw a crest and the words, '*Victoria Line /Burdale Data Storage Merge. Restricted: Level 5 Clearance*.'

Inside the file was one sheet of paper. It looked like an index, but Toby was a zoologist, not a local historian and the entries meant little to him. Under a heading 'Operations':

'*... 1948 Garton Crossing Incident: Memo to Downing Street and Security Service Chiefs. EYES ONLY*.'

He leafed through some other files until the name on a fat folder stopped him. He knew what this was:

'*Beeching- Version 1. EMBARGOED EMBARGOED EMBARGOED*.'

The red stamp almost covered the front of the file.

Suddenly, and for the first time in his life, Toby felt out of his depth. He dropped the file and slid out of the trapdoor carriage. At that moment, the lights in the carriage went out. He ran through the darkness, his torch light bouncing in all directions. Something grabbed his foot, he fell forward, his head splitting against a corroded track on the ground. He grasped at his ankle and felt the coils of a rope. It was his rope, now lying cut and useless at the bottom of the shaft.

~

The chime made Professor Winter look up at his screen and sigh. It was another email from the irritating Mr Denton. His finger hovered over the mouse button. There was a knock at the door. 'Come,' he called out. He looked back at the monitor just in time to see a few lines of code flash on to a blue screen then disappear.

His inbox was empty.

The Last Train

by Richard Simmons

This story was awarded one of the two runners-up
prizes by the competition judges

Sledmere and Fimber. Copyright © A M Ross

A fascination with old railways is something you either understand
or you don't. Marie, my wife, doesn't. We were holidaying on the
Yorkshire Wolds in July 1976, during the famous heatwave. One
morning, I decided I wanted to explore the remains of the old Malton
to Driffield railway, which closed in the 1950s. Marie preferred to
soak up the sun on Bridlington beach. After walking for a couple of
hours, I began to think she had the better idea.

It was really hot. The sun beat down from a cloudless sky. There was no breeze to cool my burning cheeks. By one o'clock my feet were tired, I had stones in my shoes and my head ached. The way ahead shimmered and danced as the sun reached its zenith. My throat was parched.

Rounding a bend, I came upon the remains of a small village station. Sledmere and Fimber was more than a wayside halt. It had only had one platform, facing the single track, but through the tangled undergrowth I could trace the remains of several sidings and loading banks, built to serve Sir Tatton Sykes' Sledmere Estate. A two-storey brick warehouse stood derelict, with gaping windows and many slates missing from the roof.

There was no sign of the signal cabin or wooden shelter that once graced the platform but the station house was still there. It had been boarded up but someone had forced their way in. I decided to follow their lead and enter the dank, decaying interior. At least it would be cooler in there. I remembered that Sir Tatton had insisted that a private waiting room should be built for his distinguished visitors. They wouldn't have felt very distinguished these days. Plaster was crumbling from the walls. Chunks of the ceiling had come crashing down. Dust motes hung in the air.

Naturally, the souvenir hunters had been there. Anything that could be lifted or unscrewed had vanished years before. After a brief foray into the disintegrating ticket office, I started climbing the staircase to the family quarters. It looked rickety and there was the tang of rot, but I thought it would bear my weight. About halfway up, I froze. I had heard the distant shrill of an impossible engine whistle.

I hurried to the door. Outside was the same dazzling sunshine. The heat haze still rose from the track – but now the light glinted off the bright steel of a well-used railway line. I could hear the approaching chuffing of a steam engine. I stood bewildered; then felt in my waistcoat pocket for my gold hunter watch. I shouldn't have been wearing a waistcoat and I didn't own a pocket watch. It was one o'clock. I felt a sense of satisfaction from knowing that the Malton train would be on time. How did I know the train times?

I was not alone on the platform. Further down, a group of young men in moleskin trousers and open-necked shirts exchanged loud friendly banter with another in an ill-fitting suit. They were stable lads and the one in the suit was off for his first trip away from the village. The others were teasing him about the temptations of the big city.

The platform was littered with baskets of livestock and parcels. At the far end, a young boy in a sailor suit craned his neck eagerly, looking out for the engine. A horsebox rested in a siding, a heavy horse attached to it by a thick rope, with a shunter holding its head. The horse's tail swished to whisk away the flies. The shunter stood stock still and sweated.

The Station Master stepped briskly from his office. He wore a stiff uniform with brightly burnished buttons and a high neck, but seemed immune to the heat.

'On time for a change, eh?' I was surprised by my superior manner. It was as though I had a part in a play, yet had not been shown the whole script. At any rate, he answered deferentially. 'Aye, sir, so she is. Good job, too. Sir Tatton used to get into a rare lather if 'is 'orses got 'eld up, God rest 'im. If I were you, sir, I'd move up platform a way. First class'll be farther on.'

I turned to follow his advice. As I did, a striking woman with chestnut hair and wearing a long green dress slipped her hand under my arm. She wore a black lace trimmed travelling hat and a grave expression. I knew she was Effie, my devoted wife. I knew I cared for her more than anyone else in the world. I knew she was about to leave for London to visit her dying mother. We began to walk up the platform together.

'Do follow as soon as you can,' she implored. 'You know I hate to be parted from you, and with mother so ill ...' Her voice broke. She sobbed into a lace handkerchief.

'I will come as soon as I have sorted out this difficulty over the late baronet's estate,' I told her. 'Do not disturb yourself. I shall have it put to rights in a few days. Then I shall come straight up to town. I would rather go back with you now, but the new baronet is anxious that we should resolve the entail as soon as possible.'

She squeezed my hand. 'Poor Albert. You apply such industry to your work, yet you always have time for your selfish wife.'

'Nonsense!' I heard myself exclaim. 'What man could fail to devote himself to the service of such a beautiful woman?'

Her reply was drowned by the piercing locomotive whistle. Round the bend appeared a small green tank engine, pulling two coaches. Drawing into the station, it was enveloped in steam. Brakes squealing, the train slowed to a standstill. With a clanking of cables and pulleys, the points to the goods yard changed. The shunter urged his horse to draw the horsebox forward so it could be coupled to the rear of the train.

For a while, all was bustle. The porter-signalman emerged from the signal box to hand parcels and baskets up to the guard. A couple of passengers alighted and gave their tickets to the Station Master. The stable lad climbed into his third class seat, urged on by his joking companions. The horsebox was attached. I supervised the loading of Effie's luggage. In the stuffy first class compartment I kissed her goodbye.

'I have real misgivings about sending you off alone,' I told her.

'Yet I must go,' she replied.

Just then the guard called, 'All aboard!' I hurried from the train. The engine took the strain and the carriages began to rattle down the line. I was left with a picture of Effie's waving handkerchief and a hollow feeling. As I turned on my heel to leave, the platform I stood on seemed to dissolve into steam. Everything went black.

∾

'Thank God! How do you feel?' Marie asked.

I looked up at my wife from where I lay on the hospital bed and gave the question careful thought. I decided that I ached all over and my head felt like the inside of the saxophone in a particularly avant-garde jazz quartet. I told her so.

'You're lucky it's nothing worse,' said another mild voice. 'You were found at the old station. You put your foot through some rotten stairs and had a nasty fall.'

I touched my head and felt bruise and bandage.

'You were out cold,' the doctor continued. 'I doubt you would've been found if your wife hadn't called the police. There aren't many people go up there these days.'

'I believe you,' I said. 'It certainly gave me pretty odd dreams.'

I told my story. Marie looked worried. She glanced at the doctor who looked perplexed. He left the room and Marie started to fuss around me.

When the doctor returned, he was with a smiling elderly gentleman. The newcomer introduced himself as the hospital chaplain and, he added proudly, chairman of the Sledmere Historical Society. He pulled up a chair to my bedside and asked me to repeat my tale. Despite my aching head, I obliged.

'How very strange,' murmured the chaplain, deep in thought. Suddenly, he looked up and studied me closely. 'One might almost say uncanny.'

I felt the sweat on my fevered body turn cold.

'On this day in 1863,' he went on, 'the train from Fimber connected with an express on the main line which was completely destroyed when a rail buckled in the great heat of the afternoon. Amongst the bodies in the wreckage they found the wife of a London solicitor who was staying locally to sort out some legal entanglement. The records of the dead list her as ...'

His voice was lost in the rush of blood in my ears, or was it the roar of an engine? I did not need to hear him say her name.

The Diary of Daniel Duck

by Elaine Hemingway

This story was awarded one of the two runners-up
prizes by the competition judges

Wharram. Copyright © Fimber Village

The small box arrived at Malton railway station in the morning post. The Station Master considered if for a moment, before deciding it ominous enough for the father of Daniel Duck to be called immediately. Mr Duck did not work the rest of that day. With a rare smile and a nod, the Station Master sent him home to open the box with his wife.

Barely through the door, Mr Duck handed the box to his wide-eyed spouse who placed it on the small parlour table. A moment or two passed. Then Mrs Duck slowly removed the string and paper. On top were some sheets of paper handwritten in their son's painstaking script, and a sealed envelope that was set to one side. The mother handed the sheets to the father and waited patiently for him to adjust his spectacles and clear his throat.

Diary of a railway man
15th October 1900
As I pen my story, it is with the realisation that it may never be read. That no one may know of my heartache and sorrow that I may never see my homeland again. That no one may hear of the memories that sustain me as I sit in this dugout in the middle of the Drakensberg, or should I say Dragon Mountains?

I understand now that I came to fulfil my father's dream, not my own. This country is beautiful, and yes there is work on the railway as he promised, but perhaps only if he looks down from the portals of heaven will he know the rigours of my journey. He is a railway man, and has worked on the Malton to Driffield line for as long as I can remember. He believes George Stephenson the world's greatest inventor, and the railways the world's most marvellous invention. We lived in Malton, so when the line opened in 1853 my grandfather was first in the line for work. My father followed him and was overjoyed when I said I wanted to follow them both. I gave a good few years to the Malton and Driffield Junction Railway but my feet began to itch for more. I felt I had nothing to stay for.

'There's gold in South Africa,' Father had wheezed, breathless from the coal dust in his lungs. 'You'll easily find work on the railways until you make your fortune.' More fool me, I believed him.

I did get a job, in that much he was right, and yes, it is thrilling to hurtle along, sometimes more than 30 miles an hour, Pietermaritzburg to Durban, and on to Johannesburg where the gold is. But that same railway brought me to Cape Town where I enlisted in the Railway

Pioneer Regiment when war broke out. And now, here I sit, nowhere near the gold, and thinking of Ryedale.

The Drakensberg stretches further than my memories of home, and Mary James. The moaning grasses strike my senses with a melancholy longing. The Wolds of my memory had a limited horizon. It was not misted, like here in the heat of October, when it stretches almost to eternity and the clouds open in the bluest sky. I have been through the seasons here, from when the Cosmos shimmered in the April cooling, through the bitter cold of the African July winter which brought the snows of a Christmas without cheer. We froze as we did our job and tried to keep the lines of communication open. We watched the grass disappear and the veld turn brown, disguising the Boers as they approached our camps. Their leather 'veldskoene' boots and khaki clothing protect them from snake bites and blend them into the landscape. Their attire is more practical than our red coats which announce us like a guard's whistle.

14th November 1900
It is the hot season now. I regret I have had precious little opportunity to write. November, and if he had one, a man could fry an egg on the rocks. There is no shortage of meat however, for cattle and buck roam freely in the veld. A dog has befriended us and the men say she could have originated in Rhodes' country, where the railway line has got as far as Bulawayo. If I survive the war, maybe I will go there, but I'd rather go back for Mary James. I allow myself to hope she waits for me in Ryedale. I should have pushed my suit against the fool who pursued her. But I started my travels thinking her lost to me. The news of her detachment from him came too late. I had missed my chance.

2nd December 1900
Here I am again, in another dugout, the dog still beside me. She is not like our collie, Jess, but she has fattened up somewhat since

developing a taste for maize meal. She is a good companion. I've called her Tess and she follows me everywhere. We've had a few skirmishes and so far I have been lucky. One of my mates was shot at Bothaville after our Major Hickie saved the day with a bayonet charge. That was in November. I keep thinking of the snow that must surely be now covering the Wolds. I wish I was back home.

If Father could see me now I feel sure he would change his mind about the big adventure. I was young with big dreams when I started on the Malton to Driffield line. I met Mary James at Sledmere station in May of 1890. I had overseen some work on the ladies' Waiting Room and was inspecting the job when I found her there. I knew it wasn't done to talk to a young maid, but she looked so awfully pretty, and lonesome, sitting there with her ankles showing above the dainty little boots she wore under the long blue skirt that matched her eyes. When she replied to my, 'How do you do?' I knew I could have listened to her voice for ever. It was music, like the notes above the middle C on my grandmother's piano. It was not proper for her to be sitting alone and no train due for a while. I asked her if she'd like me to stay in case some lout came in and bothered her.

She would be very pleased if I did, she said, but she made sure to tell me that her young man was a groom up at Sledmere House. Bringing her to the station in a trap, the pony had lost a shoe. She had insisted on his going back to the big house while she waited for the train to Malton alone. A real friendship was struck that day, and though after a cursory check of the new benches, I had no railway business in the ladies' Waiting Room, we spoke for almost an hour. When her companion returned, he was a most unpleasant sort, evidently thinking himself better than me. But sweet Mary James gave him a hard look when he told me to shove off. I watched them climb into the carriage together. He looked like thunder when she waved at me as the train pulled out.

I have told Tess about her and she seems to understand. Perhaps she, too, has memories of someone who used to belong to her. I met Mary a few times after that. Sometimes I could only watch if the groom fellow was with her, but other times she would let me sit with her in her carriage as she travelled from Fimber to Malton where her grandmother lived. I was usually travelling to Wharram or North Grimston. I suppose I could have been out on my ear if the gaffer ever found out, but that didn't happen. One day she told me the groom had proposed. I am ashamed to recall that pride and anger did not allow me to even ask about her feelings on the matter. I simply left.

There was a letter waiting when I docked in Durban. Mary did not marry the fellow, Father wrote, and often asked about me. If I get out of this war alive, I will go back and ask her to marry me. I would even go back to the Malton to Driffield line. We could rent a worker's cottage in Sledmere. Oh, Mary James. I miss her so.

The pages had come to an end. Only the envelope remained.

Dear Mr and Mrs Duck,
It is with great regret that I confirm that your son, Private Daniel William Duck, died on the 9th January 1901 after contracting dysentery. He was buried in Pietermaritzburg and as a great friend I will take care of his grave. He spoke often of his home, his family and his work on the railways, comparing it with what we do here in South Africa.

After we enrolled in the Railway Pioneer Regiment early last year, we managed to stay together much of the time. I know that he began a journal of sorts. I enclose what papers I could rescue from Dan's belongings and trust they will bring you some solace.

Respectfully yours,
Patrick Doherty

The Signalman's Daughter

by Neil Anderson

This story was long listed by the competition judges

Settrington. Copyright © Mrs Wray

Fran's father glanced down at his youngest daughter from the window of the signal box. He smiled fondly. She was just six and would have had the face of an angel if it weren't for a slightly crooked set of teeth with a gap in the bottom row. It gave her the grin of a mischievous imp. She wore a pale blue cotton dress, a hand-me-down from one of her elder siblings, and from beneath the hem her stick-like legs disappeared into cut-down wellington boots. Her attention was riveted to the moss-covered dry stone wall. She would stay there for hours watching tiny red spiders scurry from shade into sunshine and then back again.

'Frances, come here please.' He heard his wife call the girl and watched as she turned reluctantly and dragged her feet back towards the door of their cottage.

He chuckled to himself as her black rubber boots shuffled across the cinder-strewn yard, knowing she would be skipping out again in a moment her face wreathed with smiles. His wife had agreed to let Fran bring his sandwich and cup of tea today. She would be sent on the errand with many a caution not to dawdle and not to spill a drop. It wouldn't be needed. It was a rare treat for Fran to visit her father in the signal box.

As he heard her running footsteps, he headed for the corner near the door and settled himself next to the stove in his favourite chair. It was an ancient armchair upholstered in faded brocade. Horse hair sprouted through splits and moth-eaten holes but to him, with its high ballooning back and wide arms, it was the most comfortable chair he had ever sat in.

Fran's footsteps approached, slowly now as she climbed the wooden stairs. She entered the signal box, both her hands clutching the tray, and her father watched her eyes widen, as they always did, as she ran her gaze over the machinery. She loved to hear the bells ring and to see the levers pulled to and fro, making the signals whirr and clank.

There was easily enough room for two in his big chair and as he reached for a bottle from the cupboard by his side, he said, 'Come and sit next to me, lass.'

She perched beside him and watched as he balanced the tea on the arm of the chair and topped it up from the bottle. He drank deeply and felt the welcome fire warm his body.

'What's that?' Fran asked.

'It's my special medicine,' he said. 'They used to give us a tot or two every day when I was in the Navy. It puts hairs on your chest.'

'Can I have some?'

'You want hairs on your chest?'

'No!' Fran giggled.

He tilted the uncorked neck of the bottle so that she could smell it. She wrinkled her nose and drew back.

'Still want some?'

She shook her head as he replenished his own cup.

When he'd finished his tea, he refilled his cup from the bottle and listened to his daughter chatter on about the spiders in the wall, the trains she'd seen, all manner of childish trivia. Warmth and contentment crept over him.

When Fran realised that her father was asleep, she slipped quietly off the chair and turned her attention to the machinery, walking close but not quite daring to reach out and touch it. A moment later she heard shouting and peeped out of the window. There was a locomotive at a standstill. It hadn't been there before.

She looked at her father but he was snoring gently, so she went down the stairs and on to the track, stepping from sleeper to sleeper towards the big engine. Two men climbed down from the cab.

'Where's that no-good father of yours?' one of them shouted towards her.

Fran didn't understand what he was saying but the fierceness of his tone frightened her and she raced back to the signal box, scrambling up the stairs and pulling sharply on her father's sleeve.

'Wha ...?! What's that?'

He woke with a start and jumped up. Fran clutched at his cup and saucer to stop them tumbling to the floor.

He stumbled across to haul on a signal lever, then scurried down the wooden steps to lower the barrier. Breathing heavily he returned to the box just as the locomotive steamed past. Fran heard a shout from the driver in that same cross voice.

'Thank you, lass.' Her father patted her head. 'What would I do without you?'

~

Winter came early into the dale bringing sharp frosts and scarlet fever that spread like wildfire. The once rare sight of the doctor's car became a daily occurrence. Not a single household with children in it was spared, and all too often when the doctor's visits were over, it was the thin, grey-haired woman who helped prepare for the undertaker who flitted from house to house.

Fran was the first in their family to feel ill. Her body seemed to be burning and her arms and legs ached as though she had carried heavy loads for miles. She felt a little better to be in bed and she was comforted by her mother and father's presence next to her. They took turns to soothe her forehead with a moist flannel that eased the pain. She reached out and plucked at her father's sleeve, then she felt herself drift into a deep deep sleep.

~

The following Christmas was busy with parties at the nearby Hall and many guests arrived by train. The village pub was crowded every night but Fran's father was no longer a regular there on his days off. Since the death of his youngest daughter not a drop of hard liquor had passed his lips. There was no longer a bottle stashed in the cupboard by his old chair and no trains had to stop unnecessarily because the signals weren't set.

As he'd made his way through fresh snow to the signal box that evening, he had noticed the black limousine, illuminated in the gas lamp that lit the crossing. Five minutes later, he looked out of the window and saw the car still there. The dull pool of yellow gaslight showed two figures standing beside it.

He opened the window to call, 'Has the car broken down?'

'Possibly out of fuel,' the man replied bleakly.

The couple looked lost and forlorn. He climbed down to join them. 'Let's push you away from the crossing,' he said. 'You can leave the car next to my cottage.'

Between them they heaved the big car to a safer refuge as the snow fell ever more heavily.

'You'll be on your way to the Hall. Come up into the box and warm yourselves by the stove. I'll phone them to send you a car.'

He led them up the stairs and made the call.

This was the first time he'd been able to see them clearly. Both were well dressed but the woman huddled into a fur collar which hid most of her face. The wide brim of her ostrich-feathered hat shaded her eyes leaving just a huge glittering earring and a rouged cheek on show. The box was filled with the scent of her perfume.

Before long a Rolls Royce swept silently into the yard. The couple murmured their thanks and climbed down the stairs. As he watched them from the window he saw the man get back out of the car and return to the box. He went to meet him at the top of the steps, wondering if he'd left something behind.

A smooth metallic object was pressed into his hand.

'Something to keep out the cold. Thanks for your help.'

Fran's father looked down. He was holding a handsome hipflask. Drawing out the stopper, he sniffed the rich aroma of expensive brandy. He was cold and wet from pushing that car in the driving snow. A small nip to warm him would do no harm. He sat down in his favourite chair.

~

It was more than an hour later and the snow swirled even more fiercely around the signal box. Men arrived with horses dragging heavy chains which they attached to the limousine. The animals slipped and stumbled on the icy cobbles and made little progress.

People from the village stopped to help. More guests came down from the Hall. The carol singers from the chapel arrived. At closing time the people from the pub joined in. Like moths to a lamp, people gathered under the gas light by the crossing to sing and dance in the thick snow that covered the railway tracks beneath their feet.

In the shouts and fun of a general snowball fight, no one saw or heard the express train as it rounded the curve and steamed towards them.

In his chair in the signal box, Fran's father lay gently snoring, a smile on his face as he dreamed of mysterious women wearing diamond earrings and ostrich feathers.

Then into his dream came an insistent tugging, as though a small hand was pulling at his sleeve, a small voice calling out to him.

He woke with a start and leapt to his feet, staring out of the door at the carefree group cavorting across the line, the express thundering down on them. Shouting as loudly as he'd ever shouted in his life, he raced towards the group. They saw the danger and scattered, the last one leaping free of the track as the express sped by.

Panting at the sudden exertion, Fran's father climbed back into the signal box. He reached for the hip flask, pulled out the stopper and tipped the remains of the expensive brandy down the side of the stairs where it melted a line through the snow. Then he sat in his chair and patted the seat beside him where his daughter used to sit to tell him about spiders, trains and all manner of childish trivia.

'Thank you, lass,' he murmured. 'What would I do without you?'

The Ghost of Fimber Halt

by Peter Rogers

This story was long listed by the competition judges

The early morning mist drifted across the valley where the little railway station at Fimber Halt lay. As daylight cast its first rays across the Wolds, a solitary figure walked towards the station. Anyone out and about would have seen a man in railway uniform, aged around thirty of medium height and build, who walked with a pronounced limp.

It was August 1940, and Martin Williams had been lucky. His limp was the legacy of his rescue from the beaches of Dunkirk. He'd survived and, newly discharged from the army, he now worked for the Malton and Driffield Junction Railway. He was often the first to arrive and used the solitude to reflect as he went about his work. He found his new routine a welcome change, keeping the platform in order, organising the goods picked up and dropped off by the passing trains and meeting the passengers.

In the half light, he began to sweep the platform as he mulled over the preparations needed for the first goods train of the day.

Then he gave a start of surprise. He'd thought he was alone but there on the platform stood a solitary figure, a young man in his twenties in military uniform. Martin looked up at the clock. The first passenger train would not arrive for at least two hours.

Something wasn't right. The peaked forage cap, the belted jacket, the puttees. The young man looked more like the pictures of his uncles from the Great War than those who he'd recently fought alongside in France.

He approached the soldier. 'Good morning,' he called out. 'It's a chilly one today!'

No reply. No response at all.

He tried again. 'Is everything alright, mate?'

By now, he was within a few feet of the soldier and he could see how pale this solitary figure looked in the mist.

Suddenly, the soldier spun to face him. Martin's heart lurched as he saw the look of abject terror, the features contorted in fear. He pointed beyond Martin and yelled, 'Warn Amy! …The fire from the sky! …The fire from the sky! …Warn Amy!'

Instinctively, Martin twisted to look behind him, but there was nothing there. He turned back to the soldier. The soldier was gone.

The horror of his own recent time in uniform rose up. Martin felt an involuntary shudder run through him. The fear he'd seen on that man's face had bespoken worse experiences than any he had seen. And now the man was gone, disappeared into the air. A chill ran down his spine.

He sprinted for the station office, almost colliding with Tom Walker the Station Master as he arrived for work.

'Steady on, Martin,' said his startled boss. 'What's wrong with you? You almost knocked me flying.' He stared closer into Martin's face. 'Are you alright?'

'I …I've just seen a ghost.' Martin stammered out his story of the soldier from the Great War …his full uniform. 'And his face,' he said. 'The fear on his face! Then he vanished!'

Tom put his arm around Martin and ushered him into the station office. 'Just calm down, lad,' he said reassuringly. 'Let's grab a cup of tea and get you sorted out.'

A few minutes later, tea in hand, Martin's horror had subsided. He felt grateful to Tom for not laughing at him, for allowing him time to recover himself.

'That's better,' said Tom. 'Now you're calm, tell me the full tale from the start.'

Martin pulled in a deep breath and told Tom everything that he'd seen and heard. It was as he finished his account that he looked across at Tom and said, 'You don't seem overly surprised, Tom.'

Tom stared silently into his cup for a long while and then looked up at Martin. 'It was Jim Owens. Poor bloke was killed on the Somme in 1916. He left for the front from here early that year. He'd just got married too. I've seen him a few times over the years, but he's never spoken to me. He simply stands on the platform and then vanishes.'

'What happened to his wife?' asked Martin.

'Amy, she was called. Local girl. Lives in Driffield now, I think.'

'And what's the fire from the sky about?'

'Now that's new. I really haven't a clue,' said Tom.

Martin returned to work that day, his mind going over and over the events of the morning. By the end of his shift, he'd decided that he wanted answers. He would go into Driffield the following day to look for Amy. He knew people. It was a small place. She shouldn't be hard to find.

And sure enough, the next morning within a couple of hours of arriving in the town, he found himself knocking on the door of a house on Bridge Street. It was answered by a woman in her forties, neatly dressed with a kind yet discerning look on her face.

Martin introduced himself and asked if she was Amy Owens, Jim's widow. 'I know we've never met, but I had an experience over at Fimber Halt yesterday morning which I wanted to tell you about.'

At the mention of the station, Amy's expression clouded. 'It was there that I saw him off in 1916,' she said. 'It was the last time I ever laid eyes on him.'

They sat in the parlour of her neatly furnished house. She smiled kindly at Martin and told him that she'd heard the stories of the soldier on the platform but didn't like to dwell on such things.

'We lived in a farm worker's cottage up in Sledmere before Jim was called up,' she explained. 'We'd only been married a few months, but we'd known each other since we were little children and he was always my sweetheart …He still is.' She paused and wiped a tear from her eye.

Martin told her the full story of his encounter on the platform. When he got to Jim's warning about 'the fire from the sky' Amy looked startled.

'That *is* frightening,' she said. She put a hand to her cheek distractedly and looked away. 'Almost biblical,' she murmured. He watched her deep in thought for a few minutes before she drew up her shoulders and breathed deeply. 'I think it's time I went to Fimber Halt. Maybe we can solve this mystery together.

~

The next morning, as the Driffield milk truck dropped off Amy at Fimber Halt, a gentle mist again drifted across the platform in that half-light period just before the dawn.

'Jim left on the early morning train to Driffield,' Amy told Martin. 'It was a cold winter's morning and we'd walked down together from the cottage. He ...' And here she stopped suddenly.

A figure in uniform stood in the mist on the platform several yards away.

'Jim, is that you?'

The figure turned towards them. Martin saw Amy gasp in amazement and saw tears stream down her face as she began to run. The soldier smiled at her as she approached, and then he vanished.

Martin walked up to where she'd stopped to stare at the empty platform. He placed a comforting arm around her and led her to the office. 'It was him. It was him,' she kept repeating.

With Tom's permission, Martin escorted Amy back to Driffield later that morning. As they approached the town, the train screeched to an abrupt halt. Explosions sounded and the air vibrated around them. Everyone strained to see out of the windows. German aircraft were bombing the nearby RAF station. Martin, Amy and their fellow passengers could only watch in horror as bombs rained down. Then the aircraft were gone and a grim silence descended.

They made their way into Driffield and could see that the town, too, had received its share from the German bombers. They walked in silence, downcast by the scenes around them.

It was as they turned into Bridge Street that they saw more flames curling towards the sky. Aghast, they approached to see a tender and crew hard at work trying to damp down the blaze. Martin felt shock bolt through him as he realised the heart of the inferno was the parlour where he and Amy had sat only the day before.

'Sorry, Mrs Owens. Looks like an incendiary bomb,' said the fire chief. 'Most of the house is alright, but this room was badly burned. Good job you weren't in there.'

Badly shaken himself, Martin made sure that Amy was secure and looked after before he took his leave and returned to the station to catch the evening train back to Fimber Halt. He was the only passenger to alight there. The sun was setting as he walked along the platform, deep in thought.

A figure loomed out of the dusk in front of him. Martin stopped. It was Jim Owens. The soldier turned, looked Martin in the eye, and said, 'Thank you.'

Then he was gone. Martin turned for a last look down the empty platform knowing that the ghost of Jim Owens would never be seen again.

A Journey of Beauty and Uncertainty in 1944

by Emily Smith

This story was long listed by the competition judges

Burdale Tunnel. Southern portal. Copyright © Len Cook

The sun broke over the horizon, spilling exotic lemon and orange colours across the sky. Sweet silence of serenity whispered over the dewy morning fields. A tear slipped down my face as I felt the touch of the golden locket that hung close to my heart and thought of my family. I didn't want to leave them but every eligible man was required to fight for his country even if that meant being away from home. In this new world, a hundred miles may as well have been a thousand. The devastation I'd encountered was incalculable and I prayed they would be okay.

Over the busy sounds of Malton railway station our commanding officer ordered, 'All aboard the Malton Dodger.'

Our duty was to help transport munitions and ourselves to a base north of here. Protecting this train was our new challenge. We recruited the locomotive as a fellow soldier and friend. We instantly respected the local boy.

The loud chugging of the engine distracted me from the other men singing. We all had the same life-changing scars imprinted on our brains but somehow the Yorkshire Wolds brought joy and a sense of safety to our journey.

Michael, who had become a close friend, handed me some small yellow sweets, saying he'd picked them up from a local market. Sour sensations erupted through my face like a thousand delicious darts shooting my tongue. We told tales of home but revelled in thoughts of Yorkshire pudding smothered in gravy. We could thrive off one another and sometimes forget about the war even if it was only for a second.

I loved the train. The views were sensational. Field after field rippled into what seemed like the end of the world, a million coloured crops waved and then stood to attention as though under inspection. Adrenaline pulsed through my veins. I was part of the escort to a precious cargo.

The world seemed suddenly darker. Talk and memories couldn't erase the ever-present fear of a German ambush that clung to me like my own shadow.

Thoughts fragmented in my mind as I tried to take in the debriefing from our Commanding Officer who spoke in a softened tone, eager not to be heard. Our hardest task was approaching fast.

Burdale tunnel. Its name echoed. I saw the colour leach from my comrades' faces.

The tunnel was a sitting duck for sabotage. A German battalion might already have disarmed the sentries and hidden behind the moss-encrusted walls and overgrown scrub. I thought of my family, my wife, and how we would saunter down to the fields back home in summer, not a care in the world, with ginger beer and jam sandwiches, laughing and watching our boys play. I was doing this to protect them, to keep them safe and get back to normal life.

The train slowed. The intensity of the silence seemed to grow, broken only by the melancholy murmurings of swaying trees and the rhythmic chug of the Malton Dodger's engine.

As we closed on the tunnel many of my companions crossed their bodies in prayer. I did the same myself. I needed to believe that someone, anyone, would keep me safe.

I lifted my rifle, loaded it, and took up my position. What chance that I would spot a saboteur before a sniper's bullet found me? I felt a tremor run through me as my life's happiest moments played in my head.

The tunnel swallowed us, its blackness clinging like tar. Every noise, even imagined ones, sounded like an enemy solider ready to spring out of the darkness.

Bursting into the sunlight was like arriving in heaven. This time we were safe.

The silence was broken by sighs of relief. Grins spread across faces. Some of us shed a tear that we'd brought ourselves and our precious cargo intact through the dangerous journey to Driffield.

I felt my head rise with pride to be part of the team, part of the army that had brought victory one step closer. I thought of Churchill's words, 'Never yield to force, never yield to the apparently overwhelming might of an enemy.'

We arrived at Driffield to a heroes' welcome from the locals. Not everyone was to be as lucky as we were, but we made it through the war, and were left with indelible memories of the harsh majestic beauty of the Yorkshire Wolds, with our families and the unforgettable emotions of a short but incredible journey on a train.

Return to Wetwang

by Peter Briddon

This story was awarded first prize by the competition judges

Wetwang. Copyright © Mrs Wray

'Third class single to Wetwang, please.'

The official behind the glass frowned. The traveller sighed.

'Wetwang, East Riding, on the Malton to Driffield line.'

The official turned away, and after a moment reappeared with a Kings Cross to 'blank' ticket, on which he proceeded to write 'Wetwang' and the fare in capitals.

'Sorry,' he said, embarrassed not to have recalled every station on the company's lines. 'Don't get much call for Wetwang. Platform three,' he advised. 'Change at Doncaster.'

The traveller passed over his money and moved towards the platform. The station was busy, people rushing in all directions, porters with luggage on barrows, women with children tugging at their sleeves, soldiers with kit bags.

He had sworn to himself he would not go back. When he had boarded that train for Malton, with its dilapidated four wheeled coaches and the wheezing loco, he had promised himself that he would not set eyes on Wetwang again. Ever. And yet here he was: the letter out of the blue, the news. He'd packed his things, and dutifully taken the omnibus to Kings Cross station. Duty. Obligation. They would always get the better of him.

The journey north was long and uneventful, cooped up in a compartment with six others, all equally oblivious of the person at their side. But he had a window, and watched the countryside slide by, taking him away from London, from the bricks and tarmac, the smoke and noise, and back to green fields and country villages. It ought to boost his spirits, but it didn't. In London, he had been hidden amongst crowds.

'Tickets please.'

The Guard eyed his ticket carefully, it wasn't often he saw a ticket to such a remote outpost, and handwritten at that.

'Change at Doncaster,' he recommended.

'May I stay on to York, and then go on to Malton?' the traveller asked, taking back the precious piece of card.

The Guard put his head on one side. 'You can, but you'd get a better connection from Driffield.'

'I'm in no hurry,' said the traveller. 'No hurry at all.' And he leant back into his seat and pulled his hat over his eyes.

York station had a roof every bit as palatial as Kings Cross. He watched his train steam away north with a profound sense of regret that he wasn't still on it. But his route lay farther east, and he rode his next train to Malton with a heavy heart. Each click of the rail joints marked the lessening of the distance.

If York station had been palatial, Malton's was cramped and dirty, like an old man who had passed the prime of life. The traveller left the train and looked around. When he'd been young, a trip to Malton had been looked forward to, as much a treat as a day at the seaside. In the myriad of shop windows there were on display all manner of foodstuffs, clothes, toys, and any number of gadgets; and the little boy would stare enchanted through the glass as his mother went inside to stock up on provisions.

But the traveller knew that he wouldn't recapture those feelings of excitement and innocence today. Instead, he walked reluctantly towards the short, dead-end platform from which the Driffield train would depart for Wetwang. He found a wooden bench that didn't appear too dirty, clasped his bag to his side and settled down to wait.

'Please mam, please, can I have it?'

It was the same every time. As a reward for her son's good humour, she would always stop outside that quaint shop which had puppies or kittens for sale in its window. She knew he looked forward to seeing them while she rested her tired arms on the walk back to the station.

'Please mam,' he said again.

This time was different. A puppy, brown with white patches – she knew nothing of breeds but it did look adorable – had ambled over to the window where her son was making the glass misty with his breath. It yelped and wagged its tail, as though it had known the boy all its short life.

He looked up at her pleadingly. He couldn't see the bruise around her eye or the cut on the side of her head that she had managed to hide with her hair. All he could see was his mother, the one kind, warm figure in his world.

Her resolution melted: what would be the harm in letting the boy have a pet? There was a little money left over from the provisions this trip and it would be good for the boy, she told herself, teach him some responsibility.

'Who's going to look after it?'

'I will, I will.'

'I don't just mean throw it sticks to fetch. I mean who's going to take it outside to do its business, or clean up its mess when it does it inside?'

'I will, oh please mam,' said the boy, sensing victory.

For that one time, the boy and his mother had entered that quaint shop, and the tarnished brass bell rang as the door struck the spring. The proprietor – for no other would surely work in an establishment as dark inside as night was out and pervaded by all manner of unpleasant odours – haggled with his mother over the sum for the puppy, but they came into the clear sunshine outside, him holding the young dog and as happy as he'd ever been in his life before, while the dog licked his face and wagged its tail in his arms.

That night, the young dog had settled down in a small wicker basket when the boy's bedtime had come. He had almost drifted off to sleep when he had been disturbed by the sound of his stepfather shouting in the next room. He heard his mother cry out in pain, and clutched his hands over his ears, willing it all away.

Neither basket nor dog were there in the morning. Nothing was said, and though the boy cried himself to sleep for the next few nights, he knew better than to ask. He felt sick with guilt for having sentenced the dog to death, and tried to forget those few hours of joy.

The traveller looked up to see the carriages waiting in the platform while the engine took itself to the other end. He found the least careworn compartment and boarded. The train departed slowly as if it, too, had no wish to get where it was going. After several wayside stations, it passed the big quarry at Wharram, where his stepfather had sent him to work when he was 14. He had suffered it for nearly two years, hating every minute, the noise and dust, but determined to earn enough to get him and his mother away. Then one day it had all been too much, and he'd walked away with all the wages he deserved, and taken the train through the long black of the tunnel to Wetwang.

But he had found his mother crying, bleeding, and rage flared up in him. He had hunted the man, the hated stepfather, and repaid him for every slap or punch he had meted out to his mother, for the money wasted on liquor and the puppy he'd drowned: then realising what he had done and fearful of the consequences, had taken a train to London and a place to hide.

She was waiting on the single platform at Wetwang, as she had met every train for the previous three days. The traveller had got off, handed in his ticket and studied her frail body and worn clothing before she turned and saw him.

'Thank the Lord it found you,' she said as they got close. 'We must talk, but not here.'

He took her arm and they walked slowly away from the station, up the hill towards the village, a young, strong man aiding an old lady.

'I didn't mean to kill him,' he said at length to break the silence, 'but then I had to go.'

'You didn't give him more than he deserved,' she murmured, her lips barely forming the words, 'but you didn't kill him, I did.'

He looked down at her in surprise.

'Oh, after you'd gone I nursed him,' she went on, 'like a dutiful wife should. But the days went by, and I grew to hate, and – well, the Constable did what he must, but everyone knew what he was like. He didn't try too hard: said it had been an accident.'

They stopped by the old Northfield Well where the road steepened.

'London's my home now. I have friends, a job.'

'You have friends here.'

He shook his head. 'Only memories. And you. Come with me.'

'Wetwang is my home,' she said. 'Give it – give me – another chance. Please.'

He had only bought a single ticket; had he known all along? He sighed, and put his arm around his mother.

All the way to Malton

by Lesley Hatfield

This story was long listed by the competition judges

Malton. Copyright © R Casserley

'Poor Lily, she had another nightmare last night. She swears there were actually people in her room. She kept shouting, "Oh make them go away!" I ran into her room but no one was there, of course.'

'It'll be the Alzheimer's. You'd better tell Mrs Baker. If Lily is having hallucinations she needs to know.'

Mrs Baker had been the manager of Abigail Care Home in Hull for two years. When the girls told her, she went immediately to Lily's room.

'Hello Lily.' Mrs Baker knocked lightly on the open door. 'Can I come and have a chat?'

The old lady smiled and welcomed her in.

'I hear you've been having some bad dreams, Lily. Do you want to tell me about them?' Mrs Baker asked gently.

'It's not like a dream,' said Lily, her smile faltering. 'It's like they're in the room with me. They talk to me.'

'Who's in the room?'

'There's a girl and her mother.' Lily clasped her skinny fingers together. 'They're both so upset because the girl has to go away. The little girl, she won't stop crying. Then …Oh, the whistle screeching!' Lily put shaking hands to her ears at the memory. 'The train is so loud.'

She looked up at Mrs Baker through wide, tear-filled eyes. 'Then they're gone.'

Mrs Baker put her arm around the old lady and said she would 'look into things'. In reality she had no idea what she could do. That evening she retrieved Lily's file from the cabinet, her coffee going cold on the desk as she read carefully through all the carers' and doctors' notes. By 11 pm she was no further on and was ready for home.

As she passed the dining room she saw one of the residents sitting by the French doors watching the night on the lawn.

He looked up at the sound of her footsteps. 'I fear that monster Alzheimer's is getting the better of her,' he said gravely. Mrs Baker gave him a small sad smile. They both knew she could not discuss another resident, but he was right to be concerned for his friend.

'Sleep well, Bill. Don't watch those foxes for too long,' was all she could say.

～

Two weeks passed and then three. Lily continued to see the mother and daughter waiting for the train. Mrs Baker tried sleeping pills. They tried putting her with a night sitter but nothing worked. Her disturbed sleep played havoc with her daytime routine. She became more and more confused. Her friends and the staff of Abigail House grew very worried.

It was a Saturday morning when Lily failed to appear at breakfast and they found her bedroom empty. The police were called and a full-scale search for her began.

∾

Lily walked slowly along the busy main road. She was hopelessly lost. She could ask directions, but where to? It was no use; she couldn't remember where she should be. The noise of the cars whooshing by making the ground vibrate, terrified her. Then to top it all, she was so hungry. But she did cheer up when the smell of cooked bacon wafted past her. With her nose in the air like a hungry dog she followed the aroma until she reached a little café. She told the girl behind the counter that she'd be grateful for a cup of tea and one of those delicious sandwiches. The girl smiled. She would bring it right over. Lily felt better already.

The café was busy but there was a seat at a large table in the corner. Lily thought the young man sitting there, plugged into his computer, wouldn't mind if she sat next to him.

'Hello there,' said Lily.

The young man smiled and pulled out his earphones. 'Hi. Shall I move these books?'

'Oh no, please,' said Lily, tracing her hand over the cover of a large hardback book. 'They do look interesting.'

Lily and the young man talked until the tea and sandwiches were gone. Lily seemed to have forgotten her purse. She couldn't think why she would have gone shopping without it. Her new friend, whose name was Lewis, kindly offered to pay. She wanted to go home and fetch it but she couldn't remember how to get there.

'It's no trouble,' he said. 'Why don't you tell me a bit about your home and we'll see if we can't figure it out?'

～

It wasn't long before Lily was safely back at the Abigail. Lewis sat in Mrs Baker's office receiving profuse and repeated thanks from Mrs Baker who was so happy to get Lily back she could have kissed him.

'Look, it was nothing,' Lewis said, when Mrs Baker had finally stopped to breathe. 'I'd like to say thank you to her really. I'm studying history. I've got a local history project to complete for next week. Lily spotted my books on WWII and the Hull evacuations and told me all about her experiences. She is a very interesting lady.'

All of a sudden things started to fall into place. After a respectful time chatting with Lewis, Mrs Baker saw him out and hurried up to Lily's room, taking the steps two at a time.

'Now then Lily, I'd like to have a chat if you feel up to it.'

Lily nodded eagerly.

'You've never told me about when you were evacuated. I'm really interested to know all about it, about the train that took you away?'

Mrs Baker had finally asked the right question. It was as if a light had come on behind Lily's eyes.

'That! Oh, it was terrible.' Lily sat forward and shook her head. 'All us kids had no idea where we were going or who was going to take care of us. Some were laughing and thought they were going on holiday but most were so scared like I was. I thought I'd never see my mum again, what with the bombs and all! My mum said, "Lily, stop crying for goodness sake, lovey, you're only going through Driffield to Malton." And I remember shouting really loud, "Oh no, not all the way to Malton!" and then crying even harder.'

Lily giggled a little at the idea of Malton being the other side of the world. She took a deep breath then carried on.

'I kept saying to my mum that I didn't want to go. She kept saying, "You'll have a lovely time Lily!" but she was crying too. When the train pulled in I remember climbing up her dress, clinging to her in sheer terror. A man came and pulled me from her and put me on the train kicking and screaming.'

Mrs Baker felt her throat tighten with the image of this little girl so terrified. 'Oh, Lily, you poor dear thing. What happened when you reached Malton?'

'We all had to stand in a line on the railway platform and wait for a grown up to choose us. I couldn't stop bawling so I guess that's why I was left till last.'

Lily gave sad little laugh at the memory. 'But I was glad because John Windless, the vicar of St Michael's, arrived late and so he had no choice but to take me home with him. He had a wife called Anne and a daughter called Molly who was the same age as me and who became my very best friend.'

Lily paused, smiling, lost in her thoughts for a moment.

'I had a most wonderful time that summer,' she continued. 'We went all over the Yorkshire Wolds and had so much fun. Every Saturday we rode the train to Driffield to visit the market and Mrs Windless would buy us ice-cream.'

Mrs Baker felt a surge of relief that the story, which started with such horror, didn't have a bad ending. 'So it wasn't so awful after all?'

'Oh no!' Lily beamed and patted Mrs Baker's hand, as if to reassure the younger lady. 'I was just so young and it was so unexpected. In fact, I always intended to go back there to live but sadly it never happened. My Peter wasn't one for holidays or moving out of town.'

Mrs Baker tried to stay calm but it was hard not to show her excitement.

'Lily, it's you, my darling! You and your mum on the day you were evacuated. That's the nightmare you've been having! As you've got older and your memory problems have developed, your recollection of that dreadful day has resurfaced. It all makes sense now. You'd forgotten what a wonderful time you had with your foster family. But you remember now! So Lily, this is what you must do ...' Mrs Baker held the old lady's frail hand. 'When you see that little girl again, you tell her not to worry, tell her that she'll have a great time and that she will come home safe and sound.'

Lily looked at her for a while and then nodded. 'OK, I'll do that.'

But Mrs Baker didn't think she understood. She patted her arm and left the room.

The rest of the day Lily managed to sleep. Mrs Baker went to her room to wake her for tea. Lily opened her eyes.

'Are you alright, Lily?' Mrs Baker asked gently.

'Of course I am. Why?'

'Well, you're usually a little upset when you wake up.'

'Oh no, not anymore, my dear.' Lily's voice was clear and calm. 'I spoke to that little girl. She got on the train and waved goodbye. I think she's going to be ...*just fine.*'

Smokescreen

by April Taylor

This story was long listed by the competition judges

Wharram. Copyright © J W Armstrong Trust

Laura Lydon dressed with care that morning. Her employer, Brian Welland had impressed upon her that she must appear ordinary in every way.

'If I could have found anyone else to take these to Mr Maudsley, I would have,' he said. 'Be vigilant. We live in dangerous times.'

Laura knew that only too well. Mr Churchill's speech in Parliament warning about German rearmament had caused uproar. She shivered, remembering the dark days of the Great War and prayed that Churchill was wrong.

Familiar with Mr Welland's work, Laura knew it was vital the birth and marriage certificates now in her handbag reached William Maudsley without delay. They proved the man with whom Mr Maudsley's daughter was besotted, was not George Oxford, but George Preston, twice married with six children.

Welland handed her a pound note, ignoring her protest at so much money.

'You might need it. If you go now you'll make the 10.15 to Malton. Change there to the LNER line. Buy a ticket to Driffield, but get off at Sledmere and Fimber. I shall send a telegram to Mr Maudsley to make sure someone meets you. It's a small station and I don't want you waiting by yourself.'

'You're frightening me, Mr Welland. If these papers are that important, shouldn't you take them yourself?'

'Vigilance. We don't know who's watching, do we? How could I disguise myself?'

Laura smiled. At over six feet in height and red-haired, Mr Welland was a noticeable man. Furthermore, like her favourite sleuth, Hercule Poirot, he would not dream of sacrificing his luxuriant moustache. As she prepared to leave, Laura decided to pick up a copy of the new Agatha Christie on her way to the station. She'd been longing to read it and it seemed just the right accessory to a covert assignment like this.

'Remember,' Mr Welland said. 'Stay alert. Stay safe.'

She stepped into the street. For a Wednesday, York seemed unusually busy. Keeping her head down, she hurried to the bookshop, looking around as she paid for the book. Nobody seemed to be taking any notice of her. She began to breathe more easily.

The journey from York seemed endless. At every sound she found herself jumping to look round, expecting an attack. It was impossible to lose herself in Poirot's latest adventure as she'd intended. By the time she reached Malton she was a bundle of nerves. *Calm down*, she instructed herself.

Only a handful of people alighted with her. One of them was a man so obviously drunk Laura wondered why he had not been thrown off the train by the guard. A woman with a small boy gave the drunk a disgusted look as she shepherded her toddler who wobbled on bandy legs beneath dungarees straining over a bulky nappy. When the woman also bought tickets for Driffield, Laura decided she would feel less conspicuous sharing a compartment with a mother and child and followed them on to the train.

The engine began to move, clouds of steam engulfing everything in a thick fog as they puffed out of the station. As they gathered speed the clouds dissipated. Laura quite liked the smell of the smoke as it seeped through the window. The side of the track was covered in rose bay willow herb with white bindweed trumpets tangled in the mass of vegetation. She relaxed as she lost herself in the breath-taking views. Soft rolling hills flew by, lush fields full of cows and sheep.

As well as the mother and baby, another woman shared their compartment. Laura looked at her fellow passengers. The other woman was engrossed in a copy of *Good Housekeeping*. The mother was busy knitting. Laura knew she couldn't concentrate on Poirot's adventures, not whilst living a real-life one of her own, so she focussed on the scenery.

By the time the train had stopped at Settrington and North Grimston, she felt easier in her mind and decided Mr Welland had exaggerated the danger. Although that wouldn't stop her being extra vigilant when the train chugged through the tunnel near Burdale.

Her heart sank when she heard the sound of drunken singing. The man from the platform at Malton stumbled through the door of their compartment.

''ello, girls. Wan' some comp'ny?'

'Certainly not,' snapped the Good Housekeeping reader.

The man leered at each of them in turn. The knitter put her arm protectively around her child and shouted, 'Get out of here. You're drunk.'

'Don' talk ter me like that, woman.'

He staggered towards her, his hand raised, but the train's motion threw him off balance, pitching him into Laura's lap. She screamed and pushed him away. In the melée her handbag tipped over, spilling its contents.

The mother seized the drunk by his elbow, yanking him to his feet and spinning him out of the compartment. Breathing heavily, she met Laura's eye with a satisfied nod, then wiped her hands together dismissively as she sat back down fussing over the child and picking up her knitting.

'Drat him,' she grumbled. 'Look at all these dropped stitches.'

Laura felt a surge of gratitude, but the incident had left her trembling. With shaking hands she began to repack her handbag. And then she realised.

'Oh no!' With a horrified gasp she realised the envelope containing the certificates had vanished.

'What is it?' The Good Housekeeping reader jumped up with a look of concern.

For a few terrible moments Laura was too distressed to form any coherent words, then she managed to gasp out her tale. 'Quick,' she sobbed. 'Pull the cord. We must stop the train.'

'No,' said the woman. 'Wait. I'll fetch the guard.'

Laura found herself alone with the mother and child. The baby looked scared and Laura immediately felt the need to reassure him. 'I'm so sorry,' she said. 'I didn't mean to frighten you. It's just ...'

Then Good Housekeeping was back with the guard who posed brisk questions.

'Right,' he said at last. 'I'll go and find the blackguard. He can't have left the train. Don't worry, Miss. I'll get your envelope back for you.'

However, when he returned, his expression was grim. He and a colleague had apprehended the drunk, but despite a close search, no envelope had been found on his person. 'Maybe it slipped down the seats,' he said.

Laura helped search the compartment as the other women looked on. Nothing. She fell back into her seat, trying to control the dizzy fear that shot through her.

'What am I going to do? The papers are desperately important.'

'Never you fear, Miss,' the guard said. 'The next stop is Sledmere and Fimber. I shall take the man into custody and call the police.' He glanced at her companions. 'You ladies must get off, too, and tell your story. You can catch the next train.'

Good Housekeeping shook her head. 'I'm afraid that's impossible. I'm meeting my fiancé at Driffield and we must catch the 3.15 to Kings Cross.'

'And I need to get my Bertie's dinner,' said the mother, drawing her son close again.

However, the guard insisted and, in due course, the train stopped at Sledmere and Fimber. He hustled the struggling drunk off the train, watched by the three women and a handsome man who stood on the platform. The stranger walked over and lifted his hat.

'Forgive me, ladies, but is one of you Miss Laura Lydon?'

Laura's heart lurched. This must be the man sent to meet her. 'Yes, I am,' she said. 'But something terrible has happened and now we must wait for the police.'

The stranger's eyebrows rose. He nodded and stepped back a little way. But not far.

A police constable arrived on his bicycle, having been summoned by the Station Master.

Laura found herself telling the story again, backed up by her two companions. The constable listened and then reassured Laura that a dyed-in-the-wool felon would be a master of concealment. It was no surprise to him that the guard's search had turned up nothing. He would do the job himself inside the Station Master's office.

Laura watched him stride away as fierce hope burnt within her, but it was soon quashed when she saw his expression as he returned, shaking his head.

'Nothing.' He frowned at Laura. 'Are you sure about what happened, Miss Lydon?'

Laura's dizziness returned. The nightmare was becoming insupportable.

Then the stranger intervened. 'Well, constable,' he said. 'If the envelope is not on this …er …gentleman, it must be elsewhere. Before we instigate a search of the entire train, might I suggest a search of these ladies and their belongings? Perhaps by the Station Master's wife?'

Laura was too upset to object but both the other women set up a volley of complaint. It was cut short by the policeman.

'Now then. If you've nothing to hide, you've nothing to fear.'

The Station Master's wife was summoned and conducted a thorough search of Laura first. Good Housekeeping was next, and then the mother carrying her child.

'Nowt,' the Station Master's wife told the constable. 'Apart from a few clean nappies and broken biscuits on this lady and some more magazines on that one.'

Laura stood aghast. She had failed Mr Welland, betrayed his trust. The other ladies now regarded her with hostility and began to repack their bags as they muttered indignantly. Laura forced herself to concentrate, to try to make sense of it all. How would Poirot's little grey cells have dealt with this mess?

'Nappies!' she said, lifting her head. 'That man had ample time to pass the papers to her and there's one nappy you haven't checked. The one the child is wearing.'

The suddenly sober drunkard turned and fled. The woman with

the baby in her arms turned as though to follow but the constable was too quick for her. As he barred her way, the stranger chased down and fell upon the erstwhile drunk, manhandling him to the ground.

The stolen papers were retrieved from the baby's nappy. The constable handed them to the stranger who bowed to Laura as he handed her the envelope.

'Gideon Fielding, secretary to Mr Maudsley, at your service. A brilliant deduction, Miss Lydon.' He looked at the book still poking out of her bag. 'Monsieur Poirot himself could not have done better.'

Smiling, he offered her his arm.

'You've saved the day. Now, shall we go and find a nice cup of tea?'

The Station Master's Wife

by Neil Anderson

This story was long listed by the competition judges

Wetwang. Copyright © John Lidster

The red brick station building stood at the end of an arrow-straight tree-lined lane exactly one mile from the nearest village. In the half-light of morning, Station Master Blakeston had opened the level crossing gates as the first goods train steamed through. His eyes focussed on the tiny red light on the rear of the brake van as it disappeared northwards along the curving tracks. Finally, he reached into his waistcoat pocket, pulled out his watch by its silver chain and, after an impatient glance at it, went back inside. The small booking office which also served as a waiting room for their few passengers was heated by a recently-lit fire. It flickered fitfully as the November wind gusted down the chimney, blowing curls of acrid grey smoke into the room.

It was getting lighter. Blakeston rested his elbows on the polished counter and gazed out of the window at the flower beds he had planted soon after his arrival in early spring. The colourful rows of marigolds, wallflowers and geraniums were still untouched by winter frost, and behind those were his prized chrysanthemums, their yellow and bronze blooms bobbing brightly in the early winter sun. He reached for a discarded newspaper. The headline reminded its readers that the war was now into its second month. The phoney war they called it. Phoney or not, his porter had already volunteered to join the army and had been sent to fight in France. He'd had no news of a replacement before his own call-up papers had arrived in the previous day's post.

He took the buff-coloured envelope from his pocket once more. The contents ordered him to report for duty in two weeks' time. The thought of leaving his wife and handing over the station to a stranger filled him with despair.

'Are you alright?' a voice asked timidly. It was his wife, Alice, delicate and constantly fatigued from a bout of childhood rheumatic fever. He hadn't heard her shuffle into the room. She held a cup of tea in a slightly trembling hand and wore a cotton apron tied over her black dress. The toes of her carpet slippers protruded from beneath a long skirt. Blakeston surreptitiously returned the letter to his inside pocket before replying.

'Yes, I'm fine. I was just day-dreaming.'

'You look a bit preoccupied.' She put the tea beside him. 'What's in the envelope?' Blakeston winced inwardly, his little deceit had been noticed. 'Is it about the replacement porter? You know that I'm willing to help you while you're on your own.'

Blakeston smiled. He knew how delicate she was even if she always tried to deny it, but her regular offers to take on some of his own considerable load always touched him. He reached out to take her hand.

'It's not that, Alice,' he admitted flatly. 'It's my call-up papers. The army want me to start my basic training at Catterick next week.' He watched as her usually pale face became even paler. 'Go on back to the house,' he told her. 'Sit yourself down by the fire. I'll be in shortly.'

Blakeston looked at his watch again. He realised that this was more than a Station Master's routine, it was becoming a nervous habit. Another train was due and he went outside to close the crossing gates once more before pulling back the signal lever. A soot-stained locomotive still tinged with morning dew came into view hauling four freight wagons along with a brake van. It hissed to a stop at the far end of the platform.

The station yard became busy. Horse-drawn carts and wagons arrived laden with milk churns which were left along the platform edge. After that came hand carts pushed by yawning farmhands. Bulging potato sacks, wooden crates full of cabbages and cauliflowers added to the clutter on the platform. Finally, a small flock of eight bleating black-faced sheep arrived flanked by a mud-spattered border collie. They were led by a sullen young shepherd wearing a patched tweed jacket and wellington boots much too large. He penned them into a small fold of rickety hurdles and sat down on a nearby wall to wait for the Station Master's attention.

Without a porter to help, Blakeston had to load the wagons and complete all the paperwork himself before he could get to the shepherd. When he finally received the nod, the lad got to his feet and coaxed the sheep into the wagon next to the brake van, clattering shut the door. The Station Master thanked him as he fumbled in his pocket for his whistle. After two shrill blasts the train moved away through the dense curtain of yellowing ferns and foxgloves which lined the sides of the track. Blakeston was still breathing heavily from his exertions as he walked into the kitchen. He put his cap on to the table and went over to the sink to wash his hands before dabbing at his forehead with a towel.

'I'm sorry that I was so long,' he said to his wife. 'There was a lot to be done.'

'What will happen to me, to the station, when you join the army?' she asked bleakly.

He tried to sound light-hearted and unconcerned. 'It'll be over before Christmas is what everyone is saying.'

He went to the dresser and pulled out an envelope, a pad of writing paper and a short stub of a pencil, then sat at the table and started to write.

'Who are you writing to?' Alice sounded concerned.

'To the Railway Company to tell them when I'm going so that they can send a replacement for me. We can't let standards slip just because there is a war on.' Eventually he tucked the letter into the envelope and gave it to his wife. 'Can you find a stamp to go on that and post it in the morning?'

Alice took it from him and slid it into her apron pocket.

Later that week Station Master Blakeston had to take a day off to go for his army medical examination. Before boarding a train to Driffield, he left Alice with instructions not to exert herself and to leave all railway business until he returned. 'I'll deal with everything this evening when I get back.'

He arrived home at dusk just in time to change into his working clothes before the last train of the day was due. He spoke briefly to the driver.

'Any problems?' he asked, as he looked up from the platform.

'No,' the driver replied laconically. 'It doesn't take long to open the gates ourselves. Your wife said that you were out.'

'I'm going to be out and it will be for a lot longer. I've been called up,' he revealed. The driver nodded sympathetically before turning to put his hand on the regulator. 'Will you keep an eye on Alice for me?' the Station Master called as the locomotive moved away.

~

After the long winter weeks of his Army training 564327 Private Blakeston left camp at dawn. He was on his way to London and a posting abroad, but for an experienced railwayman like him, there was a way to engineer a brief visit home before he left. There was no time to warn Alice.

He travelled alone in an unheated carriage. His bulging kit bag; rifle and bandolier of ammunition along with a tin helmet and gas mask were on the seat next to him. Between Malton and his own station he travelled on the footplate sharing tea with the driver and fireman and was comforted by the warmth from the engine. As the locomotive hissed to a stop the driver said, 'I can only give you a few minutes. I'll make it as long as I can. Listen for my whistle.'

As he hurried to the cottage, his sharp gaze took everything in. The tracks were neat and clear of weeds, the flagstones too. He felt a weight lift from his shoulders. The company had found a replacement, someone conscientious.

He walked into the kitchen, his heavy boots echoing on the floorboards.

'Alice, I've come to say goodbye. I've been posted overseas.'

The fire was set but unlit and the room lay empty and cold. A pile of letters was stacked on the table. He recognised them as those he had written to Alice. The most recent was out of its envelope. Then another letter caught his eye. Unopened, unstamped, the address written in his own handwriting. It was the letter he had written to the Railway Company to tell him of his call up. But if they didn't know ...? The weight that had lifted from his shoulders returned, like a physical load to bow him down.

'Alice!' he called again.

There was no reply. He clattered up the stairs and went from room to room but she was nowhere to be found.

Two long shrill blasts from the locomotive's whistle pierced the air. No time to search further, no time to wonder where she was and why she hadn't posted his letter. He strode back and swung himself up to join the driver.

Perplexed, he stared through clouds of vapour and smoke for a final look at the neat station as they pulled out.

Then he gasped. It was the briefest glimpse but as he stared, the weight lifted again and he felt he was walking on air. There was Alice. For a second he saw her clearly, wearing his uniform, his peaked cap on her head, holding his whistle to her lips as she waved his green flag.

Sir Tatton Cooperates

by Penny Grubb

Penny Grubb is an invited contributor to this collection

Fimber Halt. Copyright © Lime Photographic

'I shall stand in front of *Sir Tatton Sykes* and wave as he comes towards me,' Polly announced.

Her father laughed. '*Sir Tatton Sykes* is a train, Polly. It would be ludicrously dangerous.'

Polly watched out of the car window as they turned off the main road on to the long straight stretch that swooped down ahead of them into the heart of the Wolds. She *would* stand on the line no matter what anyone said.

'I can see the train,' she shouted. 'Why isn't there any smoke?'

'They're not running it today. It needs repairs.'

Polly smiled to herself. Of course *Sir Tatton* would run today.

∽

High above Polly, over 20,000 miles away and too high for her to see even if she'd been looking, someone else had repairs to worry about.

'We have sustained serious damage,' the spacecruiser's report chimed, 'and significant loss of fuel. We are stuck in orbit around this odd blue world.' A few nanoseconds' silence greeted the report. They had hidden their whereabouts to avoid awkward questions from officious Overlords. There was no hope of rescue.

The Mothership pulsed its decision. 'We have sufficient reserve for the Scoutpod to reach the planet's surface where it can refuel itself and draw on board sufficient to replenish the Mothership.'

There was a general nervy touching of consciousness amongst the crew. One in a million random planets held the raw materials needed for refuelling, but the Mothership had spoken and the alternative was to spend eternity orbiting this barren place, so they crowded into the Scoutpod and readied themselves for separation.

As they neared the planet's surface, they bounced data-streams back to the orbiting Mothership, skimming energy off their scant fuel reserve, leaving barely enough for touchdown. There was no dissent to this profligacy. The Mothership's greater range would seek out what they needed, and if it wasn't there, then it was all the same anyway.

'Readings are promising ...' – a measure of surprise – '...the planet has sentient life forms and also mechanoids. I detect raw fuel in the mechanoids. Prepare lines to draw it out.'

The Mothership pulsed an image of a metallic shape tethered to long parallel lines, swathes of yellow vegetation with waves running through it meeting with tall timber fronds, leafy canopies. Smaller carbon-based entities clustered in a group.

The crew shimmered with greedy anticipation. Beneath its blue cloak this world wasn't the barren waste they'd expected.

With the last drop of fuel they swooped in to skid to a landing on a wide stretch of metal alloy-based mineral bedrock, and were at once on high alert. A backward planet like this was unlikely to contain a life form with the capability to register their presence but it didn't do to take anything for granted.

They waited for the Mothership to open communications with the sentient life forms.

～

Polly took a step sideways, moving away from her dad, away from the grown-ups who were going at it hammer and tongs, all talking at the same time in loud voices, arguing about standards frameworks, whatever they were. Over to her right, *Sir Tatton Sykes* sat on his rails, his buffers thrust forward, his eyes fixed on the line ahead.

She blinked. Had she seen the thinnest ever bolt of lightning sear from the bright blue of the sky to hit *Sir Tatton's* cab? No, it must have been her imagination.

She glanced towards the grown-ups. The argument raged louder, but *Sir Tatton Sykes* looked ready for action. She caught the glint of the rails and took another step.

～

'Target the mechanoids,' ordered the Mothership. 'There's raw fuel inside them.'

Elation filled the collective consciousness. The mechanoids were huge, each one many thousands of times larger than the biggest of the crew, and their carbon-based interiors were packed with all

89

manner of delights. Bipedal machines, well-balanced, with grade-A fuel housed inside an oval container at their top.

'The term is "head". The Mothership depleted the last vestiges of fuel digging into alien archives, but it didn't matter with this abundance in front of them. 'Self-replicating mechanoids with heads containing top quality lipid and glial-based fuel. The native term for it is "brain-matter".'

'What is their purpose?'

'Unclear. They service the metallic beings but seem also parasitic, burrowing inside possibly to allow them to travel greater distances than they can manage on their own. The mechanoids are trained to feed hydrocarbon-based sustenance to the sentients. The mechanoid head sports light absorbing organs and soundwave detectors by which they distinguish a small range of each spectrum.'

'They cannot detect us,' one of the crew observed.

The Mothership radiated triumph. 'Protocol demands that we obtain permission to liquefy and remove the contents of these mechanoids' heads. Prepare lines. Do you have access to surface alloy?'

'Yes, we are perfectly positioned on an alloy-rich store, but we cannot move. Our own fuel is too low.'

'No need. A mechanoid approaches. The smallest of those nearby.'

They felt relief. Flying a line accurately to the top of a larger mechanoid would have been difficult. This smaller one, almost in range now, was ideal to snare and liquefy.

'I shall coerce the sentient being into agreement,' the Mothership reassured. 'We will violate no law.'

A vision was placed before them of the odd blue planet and its wealth of resource.

The Mothership pulsed its transmission. It was a communication designed to paralyse autonomous thought and gain the official agreement required to grab the mechanoid resource without risking awkward questions from the Overlords should they happen to spot the violation. The archive had shown a vast renewable supply that could have been farmed for eons, but it was so much easier to denude the planet in one go and avoid the bureaucracy.

'I am now in full control of your mind and emotions,' it pulsed at the sentient being.

The being was immediately crushed, making not the tiniest attempt to resist. The Mothership sensed its metallic shudder as the current swept through it.

∽

Down at ground level, irresistible power surging through him, *Sir Tatton Sykes'* whistle pierced the peace of the surrounding countryside cutting off the raging argument as though flicking a switch. But before the battling grown-ups' mouths had had time to gape open, *Sir Tatton's* engine sprang to life.

The group, from which Polly had wandered away unnoticed, leapt as though stung. There was no one in the cab, and anyway it took hours to fire up the engine from cold.

Sir Tatton Sykes pumped his pistons and drew in sustenance from the pulses that entreated him to believe that no harm was meant to his world; that these were only transitory visitors who would liquefy and scoop out the carbon-based matter from just one of his mechanoids.

'Happy to compensate, of course,' reassured the Mothership as its grip tightened, its message flooding through, a mind-bending deluge perfected over millennia to put native sentients at ease whilst their planets were raped and left barren around them.

Sir Tatton Sykes, being a diesel engine, was ill-equipped to absorb the subtleties of the message, but its power was irresistible. With another scream from his whistle, his brakes hissed, his pistons thumped faster and his wheels began to turn.

'What's happening! What's happening!'

The grown-ups rushed back and forth, straining to see into *Sir Tatton's* cab, torn between panic and disbelief.

'Polly!' screeched Polly's dad, drowning out the third blast from *Sir Tatton's* whistle.

Polly stood on the rail, small hand clapped to her neck as though at a sudden sting.

Sir Tatton Sykes bore down.

Polly's father barely had time to register the blank stare in his daughter's eyes as he grabbed her upper arm and yanked her backwards. And as though a connection had been broken, Polly's eyes lit up with amazement and delight at the fast approaching engine.

'*Sir Tatton*,' she breathed, raising her hand in a wave.

～

'Drat,' murmured one of the Scoutpod crew. 'The line's come loose.'

'I have the full cooperation of the sentient being,' rumbled the Mothership. 'It approaches to deliver the mechanoids to you.'

'It approaches fast,' observed one of the Scoutpod.

The Mothership pulsed its satisfaction. Alien beings across the galaxies and eons had fought back with mind blocks, lasers, potions, incantations and all manner of feeble forms of weaponry. All the Mothership ever allowed was cooperation. Every one of them may as well have displayed the instant cooperation of this one, it was all the same in the end.

Sir Tatton Sykes, fully cooperative, bowled along the line. Polly and her father felt the push of the air as he raced by.

'Cooperation!' With sudden outrage, the Mothership blasted its final message. 'It has duped us with cooperation.'

With a final blare from his whistle, *Sir Tatton* squashed the Scoutpod and all its occupants, destroying the Mothership's only life raft and leaving it to track its orbital trajectory for eternity with no hope of rescue.

Dr Duggers Goes off the Rails

by Jennifer Douglas

This story was long listed by the competition judges

Fimber Halt. Copyright © Ivan Merino

'I've got a surprise for you!' she said.

My head sank into my basket. I had heard those words before. What could Mum have in store this time? Best go with the flow. This was the trouble with being *Agony Dog to the Rich and Famous*. I'd heard Mum call me that to her friends. She'd laughed into her coffee cup and made a face as she said it, but it's no laughing matter. I listen patiently to the other dogs' problems for whole afternoons while our mums drink coffee and gossip, but my hard-earned rewards are often more of a treat for Mum. Would today's surprise be like the time I was sent to College?

That fateful day had come at the end of an exhausting week. Unsurprisingly, Mum had been ill after the sponsored walk. I had watched as she packed her enormous backpack: two water bottles, my water bowl, towels, tissues, hand cream, face cloths, biscuits, hat, coat and gloves.

'It's all about being prepared!' she had said cheerfully.

It's more about getting heat stroke, I thought doubtfully.

The six miles from Thixendale had been no problem for a fit young pup like me, but Mum had started to look peaky when we reached Wharram Percy. I thought perhaps all she needed was a large frothy coffee and a cake, but as it turned out to be a deserted medieval village, she was out of luck.

But Mum is a trooper and by the end of the day we had walked nearly twelve miles. Not bad for a little dog and an OAP.

That night, with her feet in a bucket of bubbles, she broke the news. I would be going to Bishop Burton Agricultural College! Me. Not Paddy, Murphy, Misty or Henry, just me. Mum opened up the laptop and I looked at picture after picture of rolling hills, cows, sheep, horses, tractors and trailers.

Finally! I wouldn't be *Dr D the Agony Dog* any longer. I was going to be a stock dog, a shepherd, a groom. I would learn everything there was to know about agriculture. I closed my eyes and could already see the shiny medals and bright rosettes. Dr D would be a Champion of Champions.

The first sign that something fishy was going on was when I saw Big Ted poking out of Mum's bag on the front seat of the car. He normally only left the house for trips to the vet.

On arrival we were waved straight through security and shown to the kennels to meet my classmates. I hoped Mum wouldn't get Big Ted out in front of them.

There was much talking about clipping and stripping, feet and bottoms. First lesson was clearly sheep shearing. Mum said goodbye and walked away, leaving me to my education.

I will never forget what happened next. I had been brought to this college under false pretences. Before I could bark, '*Do you know who I am?*' I was soaped, combed, clipped and brushed. People pulled, prodded and preened my body in places no one should go. I was here to be *groomed!* Had Mum not told them how happy I was to wander the Wolds with mud on my coat and a dirty bottom?

Eventually, just when I thought I could be shampooed no more, I was given a biscuit by a guilty looking groomer and put into a crate. By now I was thankful I had Big Ted to keep me company as I told him the whole sorry story.

Finally, Mum came back for us. I couldn't wait to get into the car to hide my shame. To my horror, Henry was there waiting, rolling about on his back, kicking his legs in the air in delight at my embarrassment. 'He's just pleased to see you,' Mum said. He had her fooled.

Back at home, I couldn't face the others and their questions about my day at College. I had just climbed on to the sofa to fake some sleep when Mum approached with a pair of scissors. After all that professional primping and pruning, it would appear that I still had two stray hairs on my delicate parts. Not a chance. Not after the day I'd had. Not when the others were still laughing in the kitchen; and most definitely, not without her glasses.

Now maybe you understand my lack of enthusiasm for Mum's latest treat.

Another *surprise* for me, but today Mum's friend Suze was coming to watch and I hadn't had a bath for quite some time. I climbed warily into the back of the car and watched as the countryside rolled past. We left Driffield and passed through Sledmere. I thought wistfully of the park with its red deer jumping over the ha-ha, not chased by me of course. As I came out of my day-dream, we pulled into small clearing.

All I could see were a few empty train carriages and people dotted about in bright orange vests. They all stood up as we got out of the car and Mum got my lead on. This looked serious. Was I being re-homed?

One of the orange vests showed us into a carriage. Inside, Mum and Suze looked around at all the books, pictures and maps which someone had left inside. There were pictures of porters carrying luggage, milk churns being delivered by horse and cart; even a picture of a King and Queen at Fimber Halt on route to Sledmere House. Mum and Suze seemed really excited, laughing and remembering things that happened in the last century. Could my mum really be that old? It appeared that she knew all about third class carriages whilst Suze only remembered first and second. I looked up at a picture of a dirty-faced fireman shovelling coal into the engine and knew there would have been no problem with dirty coats here. I'd have been in good grubby company.

As we all sat down on a long musty seat, Suze told us about holidays to the seaside with her granny. How they sat beside the window with a tiny table between them playing games and watching the Wolds rush by. I looked up and saw an old yellowing poster with a little black Scottie dog next to a suitcase.

'Take your dog with you by rail,' Suze read aloud. 'Return tickets at Single Rate. What about that then, Duggers?' She tickled me behind my ear.

Oh, it all sounded such fun.

Just then, I heard Mum say to a tall man, 'Two and a half tickets please.'

I sat up quickly. Where were we going? As we climbed down from the old carriage I couldn't believe my eyes. There, waiting on the tracks shiny, black and puffing smoke out of its tummy, was a real engine.

I was barking with excitement as we waited at the foot of the engine's narrow steps. Would I be asked to help shovel coal? Could I toot the whistle if I was a good boy? Could I even, possibly, take the controls? I wanted to bound up those steps and get started straight away, but knew I'd have to quieten down and sit if I was to be allowed on.

Finally, I heard the train driver say, 'All aboard!'

I raced up the steps as Mum and Suze struggled into the loco's cab, giggling like two schoolgirls. I quickly jumped on the seat next to the controls before anyone else could take it. The door was shut with a bang and a clank and the train driver welcomed us aboard the Yorkshire Wolds Railway. We were off!

As we puffed along, the driver told us all about the engine, how it worked and that it had been brought from far away. The track wasn't very long but because Mum asked him so many questions, we kept missing the stopping point. Three times we were allowed to toot the whistle and go up the track before we finally came to a halt.

As I climbed down the steps there was only one thing on my mind. What had the driver said to Mum? They needed volunteer engine drivers and it would only take three weeks to learn! That was it.

Dr D. Agony Dog to the Rich and Famous was retiring. There would definitely be room in that cab for *Duggers the Engine Driver* and his dirty bottom.

Uncode

by Claire Artley

This story was long listed by the competition judges

Burdale Tunnel. Copyright © Stephen Rhodes

I held on to the tree roots as the soil from the bank fell past me, choking me with its dry dust and scratching into my eyes even though they were shut tight. I pushed my head hard against my arms and tried to avoid letting go. Eventually the rush of mud and stones stopped and I lifted my head to see what the damage had been.

A large part of the Burdale tunnel had collapsed in on itself close by. There was no chance of anyone getting out at this end for the moment. This gave me just enough time to pull myself up the bank and try to get out of the area before being found.

My hands were raw where they had scraped down the rough tree roots and I tried not to whimper as I gripped the loose soil and lunged for the coarse grass and scrub on the upper part of the slope.

I had a long way to go before I could reach the top, and a long way from there to the thick woods for cover. The Yorkshire Wolds might be beautiful but I wished this particular part wasn't quite so steep. I had to get away quickly before drones were launched to search for me. The charges I had set hadn't destroyed the whole tunnel and those who were left guarding it would be quick to retaliate.

I fumbled in my pocket as I ran, trying to get out the small box but it was wedged tightly. I heard the distinctive whoosh as a drone was released. They were silent once they started to fly and the initial launch was the only giveaway noise. They all had the standard cameras and heat seekers, but the ones near the bases had the genetic markers too. They could focus in on the hair and skin of a person and test their genetic ID. If they matched the codes, they had a target.

I stopped to wrench the box out of my pocket, opened it and swallowed one of the small pills from inside. The impact was almost instantaneous, though the full effects wouldn't begin for several hours and I would be sick for weeks afterwards. The pill caused rapid mutations and I could feel my skin rippling with the changes. My hairs began to loosen and fall out and I rubbed at my head and arms to accelerate the process, shedding hairs into the long grass. I needed to change before the drone reached me.

Sitting down, I pulled off my backpack and spread out clothes and food to make it look as though I had been walking and stopped for a rest. I put on a hat to hide my loss of hair. I knew the drone would reach me soon to check my status. I needed to be an Uncode to pass; a human bred to be subservient, used by the bases to carry out day-to-day jobs such as manual labour and growing food. Uncodes were no longer even slaves because they had morphed into a class with no thoughts of their own, a silent pack who responded to orders.

I was acutely aware of each rustle around me and the way the shadows moved amongst the trees. I slowly munched on a piece of bread and drank from my water container. I sensed the drone as it approached. It hovered high in the canopy before making a slow sweep around me. I had to force myself to keep chewing and swallowing, looking unconcerned. I had been trained for this but still the fear was almost overwhelming.

The drone came closer and I looked blankly at it, biting into my bread. It flew slowly around. It was some time before I realised that it had gone. I had been sweating so heavily that I was cold and as I went to stand, my legs were locked from the tension and I fell down. Pushing up from the musty dry leaves on the ground, I gathered my belongings and started to walk. I had to reach the tunnels before dark when the Uncodes were never seen out.

I followed the path of the railway, staying within the trees and the dappled shade. Two hundred years ago it had been the Malton and Driffield Junction Railway and carried lime, quarried stone and people. It now transported viruses that were created in the hills beneath the Wolds. These were used to subdue captured people, turning them and their children into Uncodes, to be used by the bases.

My skin started to burn but there was nothing to see when I looked at my arms and hands. My training told me that I had three hours before I would need proper medical care. Even with that, there was a limit to the number of times that someone could take a pill. Everyone reacted differently and some never lived to take another. Others were able to take it up to five times. No-one lived beyond five. I had to get to the tunnels at Sledmere. It was going to be a push but I had to report back before the sickness took me and paralysed my breathing. I started to run along the overgrown pathway that was once a main road leading to Sledmere. There were no villages now, only occasional piles of stones amongst the thick trees. It was risky being so close to the railway but if I moved away, the trees and bushes would make speed impossible.

Following the path was difficult. Steep drops and fallen trees had to be navigated. The strength of the sun further slowed my progress as I started to hallucinate. I had to count aloud so that I could focus on the route and my destination. I was concentrating so hard that I almost missed the point where I needed to cross the railway line. I crouched in the thick bushes. I had my linestick to measure the tremors and sense when an airtrain was approaching and I inched it out so that it touched the shining metal.

The linestick vibrated very faintly and I tried to gauge whether the airtrain was moving away from me or coming closer. I didn't have enough time to wait and so I sprinted across the railway, crouching low as I ran, desperately hoping that I wouldn't be seen. When I reached the other side, I pushed through the briars, scratching my face and arms and ripping my clothes. I didn't need the linestick to tell me that the airtrain was getting closer as the railway line was now moving and lifting and I could feel the air being sucked into the train's vacuum. I lay flat and held my breath. The airtrain swooshed by and I listened to its fading sounds before slowly exhaling.

I had to start to count again. The entrance to the tunnels was near but I was becoming disorientated. Like an alcoholic reaching out to steady himself in a land that was now moving like the sea, I continued on, each step deliberate and yet uncertain. The marker on the tree was in front of me and I reached out for it with hands that weren't my own.

They clutched and turned. The entrance to the tunnels opened.

I was moved into the bay on the cold metal trolley, pushed by teams of hands and watched by multiple pairs of eyes. The lights were turned down and the breathing apparatus set on standby as my lungs began to still and I desperately tried to reach for breath. I was approaching the line between, with no way of knowing if I could come back. In stasis.

The Yorkshire Wolds Railway

by Malcolm Guthrie

This story was long listed by the competition judges

Wharram. Copyright © W R Burton

Bob and Sam, friends for many years, were what they called 'freestyling' – driving around unfamiliar byways in search of places of interest, possible adventure and, importantly, pubs with real ales on offer. They were pensioners who, in their autumn years, enjoyed reasonably good health and still managed regular exercise. On this day they had driven from their native Durham to the East Riding of Yorkshire. Their objective was the abandoned medieval village of Wharram Percy.

The Wolds were something new and different and the pair were enjoying the outing. The softly rounded hills and the steep sided valleys thick with mixed woodland looked familiar. After discussion, they decided it reminded them of the David Hockney paintings they'd seen recently, albeit a little less colourful. They were nearing their destination when the sight of a diesel locomotive parked behind a hedge brought them to a stop to investigate.

'What do you think it is, Bob?' asked Sam, releasing his seatbelt and opening the car door.

'It looks like a diesel engine.'

Sam rolled his eyes. 'I meant what's it doing here?'

'Maybe this is a station. I didn't think Beeching had left any working railway lines in country districts anywhere.'

'It's not a station. It's Fimber Halt. There's a sign.'

'What's a Halt? Isn't that a station? Where would the passengers have come from or gone to? There's no sign of a town around here.'

'Maybe there was a town here in Victorian times but it was abandoned.'

They looked over the barred gate. The diesel engine stood on a short stretch of line that led to the edge of the field and then stopped. They stood and watched, hoping someone would appear who could answer their questions but it was soon apparent that no one was about.

'Let's get on to our abandoned medieval village. It's only a mile or so down this road.'

They returned to the car and set off for Wharram Percy. A few minutes later they pulled into a small car park, where a couple by a vehicle were removing boots and thick socks.

Sam hailed them. 'Hello. Have you just been to the village? What's it like?'

'Well worth a visit,' said the man. 'You'll enjoy it.'

'Have you been here before?' asked Bob.

'Yes,' said the woman. 'We were here recently in horrible weather and promised ourselves we'd come back when the sun was shining.'

Bob asked if they knew anything about a railway engine in a nearby field.

'We certainly do,' said the man, grinning broadly. 'In fact we've recently joined a voluntary group who are trying to reopen a section of the old Malton to Driffield line. It's early days yet but we're running short trips on the engine you saw, Sundays and Bank Holidays only, for the time being, and hope for much bigger things to come.'

Sam remembered the short stretch of track leading nowhere. 'The line must have been closed for donkeys' years.'

'It carried its last passengers back in 1950, though it stayed open another eight years for freight.' The man consulted his watch. 'The 12.45 would have been the next train through, but the Malton Dodger, to give it its nickname, ran no more. Until recently, that is. If we succeed we'll eventually have a line to rival the Pickering to Whitby in North Yorkshire.'

'Good luck to you, then, and safe journey home. We'd best be off to have a look at this village.'

The friends swapped their shoes for boots, tucked their trousers into their socks, jammed flat caps on their heads and set off on the signposted footpath. It initially went downhill, traversing a slope from right to left. Vegetation on both sides of the rough, cobbled track, strained upwards towards the sun, affording the walker a view of the sky and little else.

After a few minutes the path bore left, over a footbridge and through a small copse of trees and bushes to continue across an open pasture. In the distance stood a large house and, beyond it, a church missing its roof. Bob hesitated as the old village came into sight. What was that he'd heard in the distance? No, it must have been his imagination. To the left of the path the ground fell away steeply and to the right it rose in a sort of embankment. That reminded him, leading the way on the narrow track, of the talk about the defunct line.

'Sam, do you know that Rudyard Kipling poem about the road through the woods?'

'No, I don't think so. Why?'

'Well it's a bit like that railway line. It's been running through my head since we saw that engine. Hang about …Sit here and I'll tell you about it.'

They sat on the embankment's grassy slope, bracing their feet against the path to stop themselves sliding down. The pasture, with its ample evidence of absent livestock, sloped down to a belt of trees, beyond which they could hear the running water of a beck. That background music apart it was very quiet and still, without wind noise or birdsong. Bob cleared his throat and began. 'The poem is about the closure of a road through the woods and its obliteration over the years as nature takes over again. No trace of it remains and yet, on a still summer's evening, a visitor to the woods could hear the beat of a horse's feet steadily cantering through what Kipling described as "the misty solitudes" on the old, lost road through the woods. But there is no road through the woods. Spooky, eh?'

Bob paused, looking at the peaceful scene all around them, then he recited a verse of the remembered poem. 'If Kipling had written about this area,' he said. 'It would have been Wolds, not woods and a railway, not a road. He'd have had visitors to the countryside hearing the guard's whistle, no doubt.'

'Are you telling me that you've heard the sound of the old train?' Sam grinned.

'Well, I did hear something back there. Listen …there it is again.'

As they climbed stiffly to their feet on the uneven ground they heard the unmistakable sound of a steam engine in the distance. It drowned out the burbling of the unseen waterway with the clank of couplings and the clattering and sliding of a train on railway lines they knew were no longer there. The pair, despite it being broad daylight and warm, felt cold and alarmed.

'It's probably a farmer clattering about behind those trees,' Bob said, sounding unconvinced.

'More likely a plane, although I can't see it,' replied Sam uncertainly, looking up at the clear, empty sky and then, in an attempt to lighten the mood, 'Let's move on to the village. You never know, there might be an abandoned medieval railway station there.'

'Could be. I'm not surprised they abandoned it, though. It can't have taken much money. Imagine, in a subsistence economy, how long it would take your medieval villager to save up for a ticket to the bright lights of Malton or Driffield.'

The noise had abated and the pair walked on, regaining their customary swagger, to the shell of the church, chatting amiably as old friends do about matters medieval. They were speculating that the peculiar acoustics of the place had produced the strange sound effects when, from the direction of Fimber Halt, came the unforgettable screech of a steam engine's whistle.

Sam looked at his watch. A visibly shaken Bob checked his.

'That'll be the 12.45,' he observed, thoughtfully.

'And dead on time,' Sam said.

Fimber Fiction

by Robert Shooter

This story was long listed by the competition judges

Malton. Copyright © R Casserley

Henry Proud sat with his head in his hands. He had promised his wife Emily that he wouldn't give in to despair, but it was a hard promise to keep in the autumn of 1849 trapped as he was in the confines of the dank debtors' prison, cold seeping into his bones. All his savings had been sunk into the Malton and Driffield Junction Railway, the project he'd been so sure of. Sponsor after sponsor had lost courage, but Henry had not lost hope. His employer, Alfred Dickens, was a fine upstanding man. Henry had had faith that he would win through.

But the unthinkable had happened. The last sponsor had ebbed away, credit had been refused, work had ceased. The dream was dead and had become a nightmare for Henry. With the project stopped, he had no hope of recovering his money or making any more. There seemed no way out.

'Promise me you won't despair,' Emily had told him on her last visit. 'I've been reading things.'

'Never mind reading,' he'd said. 'I want you to write. A letter from a loved one means so much in here.'

'Oh yes,' she promised. 'I'll write a letter.'

He'd tried not to expect the promised letter. She enjoyed her magazines but she wasn't one for pen and paper. And she had the two youngsters to tend on only her wage from Sledmere House. If his mother wasn't close by to help, he didn't know what would become of her.

She'd thought him foolish to sink all his savings into the railway. She'd never said as much but he knew. And yet she'd been a loyal wife, tending their two children, coming to visit him whenever she could, which wasn't often. He wished she'd write that letter. It would make such a difference to see her words if he couldn't see her.

As he sank into melancholy, Henry began to wonder what use he was to anyone. There was no way out. He would never see his beloved Wolds again, never walk the imposing slopes, gaze upon the majestic landscape. His family would be better off without him.

Then the letter came. And it came as a bolt from the blue.

Not a letter as such, more a note.

And not from Emily.

He stared at the words in the familiar hand of his ex-employer. His mouth began to gape as the warder jigged impatiently and bade him hurry.

'Your debts are paid,' Alfred Dickens had written. 'And I want you back on the line first thing in the morning. The project is full steam ahead.'

Henry had to pinch himself to make sure he wasn't dreaming as he read on. Not only was the project on again, it was set to flourish. A flat truck was already commissioned to take coaches. Could this be happening? Even with his debts paid, to have Alfred Dickens, or anyone, employ a man who'd been a convict ...

And who had paid? The note had a cryptic postscript: 'If you want to know how your debts came to be paid, ask your wife.'

As soon as he was free of the dark prison, Henry flew towards home, elation giving him wings, eating up the distance, making hunger and hardship nothing at the prospect of having Emily in his arms once again. Tomorrow at dawn he would be Alfred Dickens' loyal employee once again, but the rest of today was all Emily's.

He burst into his house to see her on her hands and knees, her back to him, as she scrubbed the kitchen floor. He took in the scene. The kitchen table on which lay one of her beloved magazines, its pages bent from much reading, the good notepaper, a pen at the ready. His heart swelled. She had been going to write to him, just hadn't quite got round to it.

She turned as the door flew open, her look of alarm replaced in an instant with a wide grin of joy. In a second she was on her feet and in his arms.

'Where are the children?' he murmured into her neck.

'At your mother's,' she replied. 'I have to go to work.'

'Sledmere House can have you,' he said, 'but not before I do.' With that, he swept her up and carried her to the bedroom.

Afterwards they sat together at the table, supping tea, smiling and laughing. Henry knew they must part soon, her to go to the big house, him to do everything he needed to do to be ready for tomorrow. He remembered the words in the note. *Ask your wife ...*

He clasped her hand and told her what Alfred Dickens had written.

She laughed again and pulled forward the dog-eared magazine. 'Read that.'

He ran his gaze across the short story. It was one of Alfred's brother's creations. He didn't want to read stories, he wanted explanations, but Alfred's famous brother Charles had a way with words and the sinister tones of the ghost story grabbed his imagination as he read on, wanting to hear the denouement and yet all the time feeling that he already knew what it would be.

'Hey,' he exclaimed, suddenly realising. 'That's the tale I told Alfred about the old works. I must say his brother has made a better story out of it than I ever did.'

'I know,' said Emily. 'And didn't I promise you that I was going to write a letter?'

'Well yes, but it doesn't matter now, I ...'

'I did write that letter, Henry. I wrote to Charles Dickens. I told him about the story you used to tell, about how you'd told Alfred. I said I supposed that Alfred had passed it on to him. I told him about the railway, about your dreams for it, and how you'd sunk all your savings into his brother's project. I told him I knew it was his craft that had made such a fine job of that old tale, but then it was your tale in the first place. And I said the sponsors would soon come back if someone with a bit of clout could show confidence in the scheme. And do you know, Alfred had kept the troubles from him, not wanting to bother him with it all.'

Henry was astounded. His lovely timid Emily had drawn together enough courage to write such a letter, and obviously in very persuasive tones.

'And now,' she said. 'I must straighten myself out before I go to the Hall.'

'Yes.' He laughed as he looked at her dishevelled hair. 'You must. 1850 will be a great year, Emily, we're going to connect Fimber to the world. And hurry home when you're done. 1849 isn't done yet, and we've more connecting of our own to do.'

At the line's official opening in 1853, Henry and Emily had three children with them. The youngest, not quite three, was named Charles.

Glimmers

by Richard Dixon

Richard Dixon is an invited contributor to this collection

Platelayers' Hut. Copyright ©R M Dixon

With the sun entering the home stretch of its descent behind him and his empty water bottle rehoused in his backpack, Neil headed for home. He rejoined the track which led away from the medieval ruins of Wharram Percy, through the fields and eventually back to the car park at the top of the Wolds.

It was a beautiful place to stroll; to relax, breathe the Yorkshire countryside and gather his thoughts whenever the world seemed to be just too hectic for its own good. In his later years he had come to find walking increasingly therapeutic and this area was bestrewn with residues of history. In the undulation of the Wolds, he could feel the movement of the ancient glaciers as they cut through the chalk. The scattered information boards brought back to life the Saxon farms, Norman barons and the scourge of the Black Death. Approaching the stile he could see the familiar track bed, the imprint of the Malton to Driffield railway which closed just as the site was re-awakening with the excitement of excavation.

The way from the stile led across the bed and on through the facing cow field. Before nature rendered it unsafe, the brick bridge to his right would have been the only means to cross the track. Neil hesitated beside it, recollecting standing on its span as a child, immersed in soot-infused steam with its distinctive aroma. He could almost feel the presence of the majestic 'Malton Dodger' roaring by en route from Burdale tunnel to Wharram station, 'dodging' the villages it served and earning its wry nickname in the process.

His attention was arrested by a small flickering orange light emanating from the remains of the hut still perched on the east side of the concrete fortified embankment.

Neil stepped down the slope beside the bridge carefully skirting the boggy stream, his footing not as sure as it once was, and spotted a sharp movement from within the derelict confines of the hut.

'Hello?' he ventured.

Silence. He edged forward.

'Is someone there?'

He could make out the flickering flames of a small, roughly formed fire. Huddled in the shadows was a girl, perhaps late teens, cigarette in one hand, shaft of wood gripped in the other.

He stared at her and she stared back, shaking a little.

'I don't care whether you're 'ere to grass on me or try it on, you come any closer you're getting this.'

Without shifting his gaze, Neil took a single step back and responded calmly, 'Neither, thankfully, I just saw the fire. Is everything ok?'

'Why don't you just get lost then?'

While no Holmes, Neil did his best to read the girl's state. Her clothes suggested part school uniform, part casual, perhaps bunked off, hiding there. She appeared to be standing on a blanket of some kind, bag in the corner; probably not sleeping here but one can of cider gone from a four-pack, so possibly meeting someone. Her make-up suggested a boyfriend; her actions suggested he had not yet shown at the rendezvous. As much as she might be scared, she looked more fed up … 'lost' was the word that came to mind.

'Okay,' he replied cautiously, 'but be careful in there. It doesn't look safe any more.'

'An' what would you know?'

'Well, I know it used to be a platelayer's hut when the railway went through here. I know it used to be a great place to come to as a kid and watch the steam trains thundering past, into or out of that creepy-looking tunnel.' He gestured at the bricked, overgrown entrance. 'I know it all seems so sadly neglected now.'

Neil expected a colourful retort but was surprised instead to witness the young lady put down the wood and relight the tab.

After a pause, 'What's a platelayer?'

'Someone who looks after the track, makes sure it's safe for the trains to run on.'

'You remember 'em?'

'The trains? Oh yes.'

'My grandad worked wit' trains, 'e were always goin' on about them when I were little. We used to watch the trains at Driffield. It were best when the old ones came in. 'E could tell you all t' numbers and 'ow they worked an' where they were made.'

The girl hesitated for a moment, hanging her head. ''E's gone now.'

'I'm sorry. He sounds like a man who was passionate about the railway and wanted you to be, too. You say he worked on the railway, what did he do?'

'Not sure, some't' to do wit' station I think. There were a picture o' 'im on t' station at Wharram wi' some rich blokes lookin' at t' plants.'

'I wish I'd had a home near the railway but it closed when I was growing up; trends change, cars were the big thing. Can I ask, are you local?'

'We've lived round 'ere since me grandad died. I like to come down 'ere sometimes. Me mam thinks I should be in school more, but I 'ate goin'; coming 'ere reminds me of 'im and me dad. Supposed to be meeting Rob – me boyfriend – but it doe'n't look like he can be arsed.'

The girl took a small purse from her bag, extracted and unfolded a piece of newspaper. After dwelling on it for a moment, she reached out with it. Neil took a few steps forward and collected the cutting from her outstretched hand.

'Me dad were one of them what bricked it up. Told me 'e scratched 'is name in one o't bricks but bet 'e were lying most prob', like always.'

Neil examined the piece and the photo of the men on scaffolding and ladders, sealing the portal.

'Wow! That's amazing.'

''E's ...' She faltered trying to find the appropriate words, a phrase she could be comfortable with, '...not with us now. 'E likes gabbing about t' railway a lot though. Used to read them magazines. Reckons I'd 'ave been a good train driver.'

'And what do you think?'

She shrugged.

'Maybe. I don't think there were many lasses driving them.'

'Not then but there's nothing stopping you now. Have you thought about becoming a driver?'

'Yeah right. No good at school, fat chance o' that.' She bowed her head and kicked at the empty can on the floor. 'Fat chance o' doin' owt.'

'There are other ways. Why not volunteer over at Fimber?'

'You mean workin' for nowt? Me dad'd go ape. Doin' what?'

'They're rebuilding the railway – quite a lot of them by the looks of it, not all blokes and quite a few young people. A bit at a time but there's all sorts to do. Maybe you could help lay some track or paint the wagons, you might enjoy it and it's all good experience.'

'What, and dig tunnel out?!'

'Well no, but who knows in the future it might be your grandchild unbricking it.'

The girl's expression softened for the first time and she smiled.

'Maybe you think I could bring t' next steam train to Wharram an' all!'

Neil returned her smile, acknowledging the enthusiasm in her flippant response.

'You never know. You could at least be blowing the whistle at Wetwang if you stick at it and by then you might be an apprentice on the mainline.'

Taking another look at the article the girl had passed him before handing it back, he said, 'I bet your dad would be proud of you; your grandad, too.'

She reached over a slightly shaking hand and Neil could see the beginnings of a tear well in her eye. Without saying anything further, she turned to the dwindling fire and poked it with the stick she had previously brandished. Soon, in the enveloping twilight, the redness returned and the reawakened fire issued a small flame of acknowledgement. With her back still turned, she murmured, 'If you see me mam lookin' for me, I wasn't here.'

Neil nodded. 'Take care; don't stay out long on your own, it will be cold tonight, there's no cloud cover and the light's fading.'

After checking the side-pocket of his bag for a torch, he threw it across to the anonymous girl along with a slightly battered flier promoting the Yorkshire Wolds Railway. She glanced down at it and nodded acknowledgement, at the same time peeling another can from its plastic yoke. Hitching the bag on to his back again, Neil headed along the wet bracken track that disguised its once ballasted state. Passing under the bridge, he glanced over his shoulder and yelled, loud enough to know she could hear:

'See you at Fimber Halt!'

Leaves rustled in the evening quiet. He took heart from her lack of retort.

The Snows of Winter

by Alan Smith

This story was long listed by the competition judges

Snow on the Wolds. Copyright © www.innes.co.uk

Bobby clattered down the stairs, hoping that his grandma had found the photographs he'd asked her to search out. He'd heard the story of Grandpa Sydney's train from both her and his mum, and it would be perfect for his school Christmas card project.

'Don't just download everything off the net,' their teacher had implored. 'Show a bit of initiative. I want to see some family history.'

'Have you found Grandpa Sydney's photos?' he said as he burst into the room.

'Gently, Bobby,' said his mum. 'You're like a herd of elephants.'

'Have you found them, Gran?'

'Found it,' she corrected. 'Here you are.'

Bobby rushed to look and struggled to hide his disappointment. 'Is there only one?' He stared at it, trying to make out the detail. 'Why didn't they take more? Why is it so far away? I can hardly see anything.'

His grandma laughed. 'It was 1957, Bobby. Sixty years ago. It's a wonder there's a photo at all. There were no camera phones in those days. Me and Grandpa Sydney didn't even have a camera until years later.'

'All that snow,' said his mum, 'and nothing but the train tracking a path through it. It looks so peaceful, but I know it was a real drama from the stories my dad told.'

Bobby took the old print and carried it to the window. In the brighter light he studied it and saw tiny details emerge. A real drama, his mum had said. That would be just right for his project, a bit of drama. But so far all he could see was a peaceful blanket of snow.

~

Syd looked out over the white landscape that was Malton station on Christmas Eve. In all his years as a driver for the Malton and Driffield Junction Railway this was as bad as he'd seen it, worse even than the winter of '47 ten years before. This one would be whiter than any that Bing Crosby might sing about.

It had been an early and bitterly cold start, but he and George, his partner on the footplate of Loco 62387, now had the boiler fired up and had rewarded themselves with mugs of scalding tea.

'We'll have to get a move on, Syd,' called George, 'if we're going to get this 'ere train out on time.'

Syd took the controls and eased the hissing, steaming loco out of its sidings. Then began the business of coupling it up with the mixed passenger and goods rolling stock that was theirs to take through seven intermediary stations to Driffield. Syd wondered how well they would manage to keep to time in this weather.

The guard blew his whistle and waved his green flag. And with satisfyingly little wheel slip the 7.05 was on its way.

Once they were in the open country of the Yorkshire Wolds, the snow began to fall with greater intensity. Syd's eyes became slits of concentration as he fought to see ahead through the white swirls of snow. But he knew this route like the back of his hand, and with George's unstinting feeding of the fire box with the coal it craved, they made good time.

Two passengers alighted at Settrington carrying a huge turkey between them. At North Grimston no one got off and no one got on.

As they approached Wharram, conditions deteriorated and Syd had to slow the train to a crawl. They drew into the station and the guard came to call up into the cab. 'It's worse ahead. There's talk of harnessing you up with another loco at Sledmere with a snow plough to get you through to Driffield.'

'Cor blimey, that'll be a first for us,' Syd called back to George.

As they eased out of Wharram, Syd glanced at the clock. 'Four and a half minutes late,' he told George. 'That's not bad in this lot, but goodness knows how late we'll be at Driffield.'

They headed on through the whiteout to Burdale where the Station Master told them, 'Another loco with a snow plough attached managed to reverse up from Driffield before things got this bad. It'll be waiting for you in Sledmere and Fimber.'

'We'll not only be the first train through to Driffield today,' said Syd, 'but likely the last.'

From Burdale to Sledmere, Syd thought the intensity of the falling snow eased off, but the sky was white where an easterly gale forced the huge flakes directly at him and George, stinging their faces as they tried to peer ahead. The signals were all set right for them and they kept up a steady pace. Plumes of smoke and steam distinguished themselves from the swirling snow as they neared the station at Sledmere and Fimber. A Standard 73156 with snow plough was waiting to ease their journey on through the unforgiving Yorkshire Wolds to their destination.

Sydney eased his charge up behind the steam-belching monster and within minutes they were coupled and ready to leave.

They heard the guard's piercing signal and just made out a flash of green in the white swirl. The tandem locos hissed and grunted as they pulled out of the station to be swallowed into the white landscape.

As the two trains made their way through the snow, the blinding whiteness eased and a pale sun emerged from behind the clouds. The vista ahead became a carpet of a million diamonds that shone and glistened with brilliant intensity.

The noise of an engine broke Syd's concentration. Surely no other vehicle could be out and about in this lot. It took a moment for him to identify the source, then he looked up to see a small plane approaching.

George had seen it too. 'Not the best of days to be up there,' he called.

'Not the best of days to be down here either,' countered Syd, adding, 'What do you think he's doing out and about on such a day?'

They stared upward as the plane came close and could distinguish a figure leaning from a side window.

'Looks like some fool is up there with a camera taking photographs,' said George. 'Whatever do you think he's doing a daft thing like that for?'

They exchanged glances and gave sorry shakes of their heads for this foolhardiness, but the antics of this aerial so-and-so weren't their concern. They had a train to get through to its final station.

The clouds had covered the sun once more by the time they arrived in Wetwang, and as they pulled out to head for their penultimate stop the snow began to fall with added vigour. There were no passengers at Garton and with the good wishes of the station staff, they set off again on the final leg of their journey to the accompaniment of the shrill of the whistle. A layer of snow settled on the guard's hat as he waved them on to their final destination.

As Driffield and the end of the line came into sight, Syd and George exchanged a grin.

'We've not done so badly all things considered,' Syd said, looking at the clock.

Once the two locomotives came to a halt and all the passengers had alighted, Syd and George climbed down to go and join the colleagues who had been at the controls of 73156 in a welcome and festive nip at the end of a hard shift.

George looked at the clock. 'We didn't do badly for time,' he said. 'And all souls safe and sound.'

Syd glanced up at the sky. 'Let's hope that damned fool in the plane made it back too.'

～

'It was printed in the newspaper, that photo,' Bobby's grandma said.

'He often talked about it,' added his mum. 'My dad and the train he took through the snow. It was the only one that made the journey from Malton to Driffield that day.'

As Bobby studied the picture closely, the details were revealing themselves. 'Wow,' he said suddenly. 'Just look at the size of the snowball the train is making.'

Other than that line of engines and carriages, it was an empty landscape, thick with snow. They were completely alone. No cameras, no phones. They'd both been wrong when they said the photo looked peaceful. As he studied it, the excitement of that long perilous journey leaked out of the picture and settled in his head.

'This is going to be the best project ever,' he said as he rushed back to his room to get started.

Posh Girl from London

by Drew Wagar

Drew Wagar is an invited contributor to this collection

Sledmere and Fimber. Copyright © Mike Mitchell

Briony looked out of the car window, her own face half-mirrored in the reflection. Rain was slashing the pane, water droplets streaming backwards. The sky was grey and overcast. She slumped in the rear passenger seat trying to ignore the irritating tinkling sounds coming from her brother's head-phones.

Bored, bored, bored …

They'd turned off the motorway at least. Now they were driving along undulating lanes which got narrower and narrower as they progressed. Dreary looking green hills stretched as far as she could see. It looked cold, damp and uninviting.

Two weeks. I can't do it!

She saw a sign marked 'Burdale'. Her mother turned around in the passenger seat.

'Nearly there, pack up your stuff.'

Briony rolled her eyes. Two weeks stuck at her grandmother's house. No wifi, no phone signal. Not even a TV!

Going to be the worst holiday ever.

It didn't get any better when they arrived. The rain was still lashing down. The house was cold. Her parents got a cup of tea, but there were no fizzy drinks, just some orange squash, so weak she'd have actually preferred water.

Her grandmother was just as she remembered. Old clothes, wrinkles, tiny spectacles perched upon a long pointed nose.

Old woman smell ... Ugh.

The house smelt just as bad – like a museum, all old polish and manky slippery rugs spread on a floor that creaked wherever you walked. There was nothing interesting in the slightest. No DVDs, nothing, only a bunch of old books. The kitchen didn't even have a microwave, just some massive iron thing her grandmother referred to as a 'range'. You had to shovel coal into it.

Her brother loved it.

She was shown to her room, which had a bed, a bookcase, a bedside table and a lamp. No TV. No spare socket. Not even a radio.

It's the dark ages. Can't even charge my iPad.

The evening meal was some splodgy brown mess with far too many vegetables and some mashed potatoes. She pushed it around her plate until she was told off by her mother.

'Briony, eat up,' she whispered fiercely. 'It's good wholesome food.'

I just want KFC!

Briony put on her best scowl.

'Eat it.' Her mother's false smile promised later punishment if she didn't comply. Briony wasn't feeling cooperative.

'I don't want it, I don't like it!'

'Briony!'

'I didn't want to come on this holiday. I hate this place and I hate all of you!'

She knew she'd gone too far. She didn't need her father's thunderous voice to tell her. She was banished to her bedroom and the door slammed behind her.

'...always sulking, never satisfied! All the things we do for her, she's never grateful ...'

She cried then, out of sheer frustration and humiliation more than anything else. No one came to see her. She heard laughter later on and the clink of drinking glasses, but then the lights were switched off.

Gone to bed without even seeing me! Nobody cares.

The next day she was awoken by the strangest sound. It was as if a hundred birds had gathered outside the window of her room and were deliberately making a din to get her up. She pulled back the faded curtains and squinted in the bright sunshine.

The sight of a green valley dotted with trees with the morning sunlight blazing upon it was a welcome change to the drab grey she had expected. The birds were sitting in a tree just down from the house. There were dozens of them, all chirping loudly. She pushed her finger around the condensation on the cold window pane.

Briony heard her stomach rumble. It was freezing too, so she got dressed and headed down the creaky stairs, half noticing the old photos that lined the walls.

Black and white. Old people in stupid clothes.

One caught her eye. A girl with stupid ponytails, dressed in a petticoat, standing in front of a dirty old train. She was waving a flag. The photo frame had a label, 'The Malton Dodger'.

Whatever.

She walked into the kitchen, glad of the warmth.

It was empty apart from her grandmother, who was fussing over the range. She turned as Briony entered.

'Awake I see,' her grandmother said, favouring her with a stern look.

Briony could do looks too, and scowled back.

'Your parents and your brother have gone out for the day,' her grandmother said. 'You're ...'

'What?' Briony exclaimed. 'They didn't take me?'

Her grandmother placed a bowl of something steaming in front of her along with a spoon.

'After your behaviour last night I can't blame them,' her grandmother said. 'In my day I'd have got the cane for such insolence.'

That caught Briony's attention. 'You were caned when you were young?'

'Oh yes, I was quite the little tearaway,' her grandmother said. 'Got what I deserved. It was fair, mind.'

Briony turned her attention back to the bowl. It smelt nutty.

'What is this?'

'Porridge.'

'Porridge?'

'Fill you up and good for you, to boot.'

Briony tentatively tried a spoonful. It was creamy and warm. Ok-ish, though not very sweet.

'So, what are you going to do today?' her grandmother asked.

Briony shrugged. 'Dunno.'

'Well, you can't stay here all day. I'm walking to the market for groceries.'

'How far is it?'

'Three miles or so.'

'Three miles! Haven't you got a car?'

'Now why would I want all the expense and hassle of a car?' her grandmother answered. 'It's only an hour's walk in the sunshine, cake and a chat with my friends and then an amble back. What could be lovelier than that?'

Costa with my mates, hanging at the mall, PS4, facebook …

Briony decided to change the subject, she didn't think her grandmother would appreciate the list.

'So, what is there to do?'

'Well, you could read some books, play in the garden …'

Play in the garden? I'm not a child …

'…or you could walk down to the old railway station. That's a lovely walk. I used to go that way when I was your age.' Her grandmother sighed. 'Trains have long gone of course, used to be wonderful to see them huffing and puffing along the line ...'

Briony's attention started to wander.

Might as well, nothing else to do …

Somehow she ended up outside, blinking in the sunshine, with a bag full of pastries, meats and biscuits, a bottle of squash and some vague directions. Her grandmother shooed her off and walked away up the road.

❧

She couldn't have taken the right route, but she eventually found what she assumed was the railway line. She wandered down the embankment, her trainers slipping on the damp grass. It was steeper than it looked and she had to run to keep from losing her footing.

She arrived at the bottom thinking there was something rather strange about it. It was dead straight in one direction. There before her was a broken down old building, sitting just above a tatty looking section of raised concrete.

Must be the station.

A quick scramble through the nettles and brambles got her, with a few scratches, to the old place. It was in a poor way. The roof had fallen in and everything inside that she could see was covered in damp, mould and other rotting stuff. There was no glass left in the windows and the wind blew through the shell of bricks with an eerie whistling.

She walked down the length of the platform, trying to imagine what it would have been like in its heyday. It was hard. There was no railway track for starters, just a faint depression in front of the platform, now full of bushes and brambles.

There was a bench, rotten at one end, but somehow solid at the other. After a quick test she sat down on it and began to munch through some of the biscuits her grandmother had packed. They were nutty too, but tasted surprisingly good, leaving a rich and honey-like taste on her tongue. The sunshine was warm about her.

Actually is nice here …

She looked around with wider eyes. Birds were singing in the branches as leaves rustled in the breeze. Wildflowers were spotted about her, growing up through cracks in the paving. Above, the blue sky was dotted with fluffy clouds slowly drifting. She could smell something sweet.

Something was sticking up at the end of the platform. She couldn't make it out exactly, so she put down the bag and wandered towards it.

It was a sign.

It was tarnished and worn, but she rubbed away the mildew and was rewarded with readable letters.

Passengers must not cross the line.

Well. That hardly mattered now did it? There wasn't a 'line' after all. Maybe there was something more interesting on the other side. Adults always put up signs to stop you going into interesting places.

Briony walked past the sign without a second thought.

'Hey! You! What the devil are you playing at?'

She jumped at a voice, a deep rumble and a shrieking whistle, as if something huge was working its way towards her. She spun around, ready with excuses, her heart thumping in her chest. It had come from behind her, the voice thick with a Yorkshire accent.

There was nothing there.

The platform was just as deserted as before. There was no one there.

She could feel her heart hammering in her chest, thumping hard and fast. She couldn't have imagined it.

The wind blew louder, a whistling cry through the building that almost sounded like ...

She found her arm wrenched, and staggered to one side.

'Can't you read?'

She looked up into the face of an angry red-faced man dressed in some kind of uniform. She only caught a brief sight of a brass badge with the words 'Station Master' on it before ...

'Bloody children,' he said. 'Where's your ma and pa ...? Eh? I'd like to give 'em a piece of my mind!'

'They're out,' Briony stammered, bewildered.

'Not from 'round these parts are you?' the man asked. 'You going somewhere? Got a platform ticket maybe?'

'Er ...'

'Not with you, I suppose,' the man said. 'Your wits neither, I'll warrant. Stand back will yer? The train's due in any moment!'

He pushed her backwards.

Her mouth fell open.

Gone were the weeds and the cracked old surface of the platform. Restored were rows of brightly painted benches, signs, flowers, glass and even lights shining from the windows of the old station. Before the platform were two parallel lines of the railway track, glowing bright in the sunshine.

And the noisy chatter of conversation.

The platform was heaving with people, young and old, with children weaving about between them, holding flags. They were all dressed in the most bizarre clothes Briony had ever seen. Flat caps, stockings and breeches for the men, with the occasional top hat to mix things up. All the women wore long dresses, some flowery, with bonnets and straw hats.

She blinked, looking about her in amazement, trying to get her bearings.

What is going on?

No one seemed to be looking at her fortunately. She quickly looked down at her jeans and trainers, and her M&S fleece before staggering backwards to sit upon the bench she had been on before, only now it was miraculously fixed.

'What are you dressed as?' said a giggly voice. 'A sailor?'

Briony turned to see another girl sitting next to her. She was dressed in a … well, a dress, with a petticoat and pinny, her hair in a severe centre parting, tied in ponytails and decorated with bright pink ribbons. A flag was clutched in her hand.

'No,' Briony retorted. 'You're the one who's dressed up.'

'Are you foreign, like?' the girl said. 'You talk funny. My da says foreigners are trouble and make all the wars. What about you?'

'I'm not a foreigner. I'm from Kent.'

'Kent? Where's that?'

'In the south … near London.'

'London!' the girl exclaimed. 'Are the streets really paved with gold? Oh, do say they are! Are you rich?'

'What?'

They were interrupted by cheers. Both looked around to see the crowds of people on the platform surge forward, looking to their right and waving their flags.

'It's the Malton Dodger!' the girl exclaimed.

'The what?'

'That's what I'm calling it. It's dodged us long enough but now it's here. Come on!'

Briony found herself wrenched to her feet and dragged across to the platform edge. They were just in time to see a huge engine roll alongside the platform, thick black smoke churning around it, accompanied by the clank and rumble of tonnes of heavy metal. Briony jumped as a loud whistle, and a huge cloud of steam, erupted from the engine as it came to a halt right next to them.

The girl was jumping up and down, waving her flag madly. She turned to look at Briony with a wide grin on her face.

'Have you ever seen the like?' she said. 'Now we have our very own railway line. It's been so many years waiting! Da says it will bring jobs and money and all manner of wonderful things.'

'It's only a train ...' Briony said, but her voice dropped as she continued to watch. The driver of the train was shaking hands with dozens of people who were crowding around trying to get near him as if he was some kind of celebrity. She looked back at the station to see a huge banner.

'Grand Opening.'

I've gone mad ... or I'm dreaming ... or both!

'The newspaper men! Look!'

Briony was dragged around again, to be confronted with a series of severely dressed men holding a series of box-like contraptions.

'Hold still!'

About her everyone stood stock still. She got a brief impression of expectation before a blinding flash went off, dazzling her.

She blinked, unable to see for a moment. She staggered back, thinking to put her hand out against the train to balance herself.

But there was nothing there and she tumbled off the platform to lie, slightly winded, on the grassy hummock below.

Birds sang, trees rustled.

She slowly got to her feet. The train, the crowds, the banner and the girl had all disappeared. She was standing on the old track bed, in the weeds and brambles.

Alone.

There was just the bench and her bag.

She leapt back on to the platform, looking around her, calling out. But there was no answer. The girl with the pink ponytails was gone.

She grabbed the bag and ran.

~

Her grandmother was already back home. Briony could hear the old kettle whistling away on the range.

'Hello there, did you …? Well I never!'

Briony raced past and pounded up the stairs, skidding to a halt halfway up. The old black and white photo still hung on the wall. She looked closely at it.

The girl was standing where she had been before, waving her flag in front of the old train. Only now she could see that it wasn't an old train, it was shiny, new, with polished brass work and fittings.

Exactly like …

She peered closer. There was another figure next to the girl. A rather dour looking figure she had first taken for a boy, half in the shadow and a bit blurred by the old camera. Whoever they were they hadn't stood still enough.

Briony gasped, feeling her heart thumping in her chest.

'Lovely old picture, isn't it? It was quite a thing to have a photograph back then.'

Briony turned to see that her grandmother had stepped up behind her.

'Who is the girl with the ponytails?' Briony managed to whisper.

Her grandmother smiled. 'Oh, that's my nan. Your great-great-grandmother I suppose. This picture was taken in 1853 you know. She was a pretty little thing wasn't she?'

'Great-great-grandmother …' Briony mouthed.

'It was the opening day of the railway,' her grandmother said. 'Nan used to tell all these funny stories you know. She said she'd met a posh girl from London on the train. She certainly knew how to spin a yarn …'

Posh girl from London?

'The railway, can you tell me more about it?'

'Well, I've got a book somewhere … look, here it is.'

There was a small bookshelf running the length of the staircase wall just above the photos. Her grandmother reached up and pulled out a dusty hardback book.

Briony took it, looking over the cover.

The Yorkshire Wolds Railway, a history.

Briony looked up at her grandmother.

'Can you tell me more about her? Your nan? What happened to her?'

'Well, now then. That's a bit of a tall order. I'll need a sit down and a cup of tea for that.'

'I'll get it!'

Briony raced down the stairs and was into the kitchen like a flash. Her grandmother made her way down rather more sedately, chuckling as she went.

Afterword by Mark Blakeston, Mayor of Driffield

As Mayor of Driffield I was keen to back an initiative that supported the aims of the Yorkshire Wolds Railway of informing and educating people about the former line and that drew upon our area's rich cultural heritage. Driffield has made its mark in the world of the creative arts – it was home to some of the country's great artists such as Benjamin Fawcett (1808-1893) one of the finest English woodblock colour printers; literary giant Winifred Holtby (1898-1935) who is said to have conceived her blockbuster, South Riding, as a result of an evening spent in Driffield; and David Bowie's drummer, Mick Woodmansey, who was born (1951) in the town. So what better way to bring the Wolds alive than by tapping the creative flair of modern-day enthusiasts?

The range of this anthology is remarkable. Some of the stories are pure fiction, some are based on fact; they are all entertaining. They chart the Wolds and the Malton to Driffield railway line from its inception in the 1850s through to the present, and on into the future. Wonderful and painstaking detail is alternated with views from a distance as we are not only shown the natural beauty of the Yorkshire Wolds, but a touch of the supernatural as well.

One of my last duties as Mayor in 2017 was to help present the prizes to the worthy winners of this competition. I congratulate the authors for their excellent contributions, the volunteers of the Yorkshire Wolds Railway for their hard work and innovative ideas, and Fantastic Books Publishing for the production of this high quality anthology. I hope it will inspire others to find out more and visit this great region.

Councillor Mark Blakeston, Mayor of Driffield 2016–2017.

We sincerely hope you enjoyed these stories and will get online and let our authors know by leaving them a review on Amazon and Goodreads.

You can find more delightful tales and wonderfully woven prose at our Fantastic Books Store.

www.fantasticbooksstore.com/

Dreaming of Steam arose from a short story competition run jointly by Fantastic Books Publishing and the Yorkshire Wolds Railway, and sponsored by the Authors' Licensing and Collecting Society. For full details please visit the competition site at tinyurl.com/YWRComp

About the Yorkshire Wolds Railway

The new Malton Dodger. Copyright © Richard Dixon

The rolling chalk hills of the Yorkshire Wolds, home to acres of unspoilt countryside, small villages and bustling market towns, extend in an arc from the golden sand of the North Yorkshire coast to the banks of the Humber. It is a region steeped in history with notable archaeological remains and inspiring landscapes.

A railway between Malton & Driffield was first proposed in 1845. John Birkinshaw (pupil of Robert Stephenson) and Alfred Dickens (younger brother of Charles Dickens) were appointed to oversee construction and despite numerous financial and engineering setbacks the Malton & Driffield Junction Railway opened in 1853. For a century, the railway wove its way through the heart of the Wolds, its passenger service known locally as the 'Malton Dodger'. What better way to savour the beauty of the landscape and wonderful Yorkshire panoramas than by rail?

With the closure of local quarries and increased popularity of motor transport, the railway eventually fell into decline. Passenger services were withdrawn in June 1950 and the line finally closed in 1958. The track was soon dismantled and stations were sold or left to nature.

Half a century later with the track-bed still discernible for most of its route, a band of enthusiasts shared a vision to restore part of the railway as a heritage attraction. Thus, the Yorkshire Wolds Railway – the only heritage railway in East Yorkshire – was born.

Open Day at the Yorkshire Wolds Railway. Copyright ©Richard Dixon

With an ever-growing number of zealous volunteers and plenty of hard work, the Yorkshire Wolds saw its first loco run again in 2015. Renamed 'Sir Tatton Sykes' after the generous support of the current baronet of Sledmere estate on whose land it operates, a revitalised diesel loco has provided rides on a short stretch of line at 'Fimber Halt', close to the site of the former Sledmere and Fimber Station.

There is a long way to go to fulfil the vision of a line once more offering passenger services through the heart of the Yorkshire Wolds but at the time of production of this book, it is beginning to progress southwards.

Yorkshire Wolds Railway would like to thank all those who took part in the competition and Fantastic Books Publishing, without whom this anthology would not be possible. We hope that the stories it contains will inspire you to come to the Yorkshire Wolds, to visit the railway or even get involved.

Thanks must also go to all the volunteers for their contributions and considerable achievements to date and in the future.

As a result of those efforts, we can all be dreaming of steam.

Fimber Halt. Copyright ©Richard Dixon

We will be delighted if this collection inspires you to visit the
Yorkshire Wolds Railway either in person at
Fimber Halt
Beverley Road
Fimber
YO25 3HG
Tel: 01377 338053
or in the virtual world on
Facebook www.facebook.com/ywrailway and
Twitter @YWRailway

The site in winter. Copyright © msh.co.uk 2013 – Michael Hopps Photographer

www.yorkshirewoldsrailway.org.uk/
www.localgiving.org/charity/yorkshirewoldsrailway

www.ingramcontent.com/pod-product-compliance
Lightning Source LLC
Chambersburg PA
CBHW061826040426
42447CB00012B/2838